Every Day Counts

Every Day Counts

*Lessons in Love, Faith, and Resilience
from Children Facing Illness*

Maria Sirois, Psy.D.

Walker & Company
New York

Copyright © 2006 by Maria Sirois

First published in the United States of America in 2006 by
Walker Publishing Company, Inc.
Distributed to the trade by Holtzbrinck Publishers

For information about permission to reproduce selections from
this book, write to Permissions, Walker & Company,
104 Fifth Avenue, New York, New York 10011.

Library of Congress Cataloging-in-Publication Data

Sirois, Maria.
Every day counts : lessons in love, faith, and resilience
from children facing illness / by Maria Sirois.
p. cm.
Includes bibliographical references.
ISBN-13: 978-0-8027-1495-4 (hardcover)
ISBN-10: 0-8027-1495-1 (hardcover)
1. Cancer in children—Patients—Care. 2. Cancer in children—
Psychological aspects. I. Title.
RC281.C4S53 2006
618.92'994—dc22
2005031063

"In Blackwater Woods" copyright © 1983 by Mary Oliver, from
American Primitive. Reprinted by permission of the author.

Visit Walker & Company's Web site at www.walkerbooks.com

Typeset by Westchester Book Group
Printed in the United States of America by Quebecor World Fairfield

2 4 6 8 10 9 7 5 3 1

For the children,
and those who love them

. . . Every year
everything
I have ever learned

in my lifetime
leads back to this: the fires
and the black river of loss
whose other side

is salvation,
whose meaning
none of us will ever know.
To live in this world

you must be able
to do three things:
to love what is mortal;
to hold it

against your bones knowing
your own life depends on it;
and, when the time comes to let it go,
to let it go.

**—from "In Blackwater Woods" by
    Mary Oliver**

Contents

Introduction

The Choice of an Open Heart

There are moments in life when the forces that be hit us over the head and say, "Here. Now. Pay attention. This is important." Infants arrive, towers fall, homes burn, lost ones return, illness erupts, children die—such moments carry with them a potency and a possibility. In these concussive moments we are left with a choice: to open our hearts and gather what wisdom we can or to shut down and in effect, walk away. In "The Summer Day" poet Mary Oliver challenges, "what is it you plan to do with your one wild and precious life?" The question streaks like an arrow shot through time from the voices of mystics, philosophers, and writers. In *The Writing Life* Annie Dillard answers, demanding that we "play it, lose it, all, right away, every time," and from centuries back Gerard Manley Hopkins, Jelaluddin Rumi, and Kabir offered the same sentiment. In "The Time Before Death" Kabir wrote:

> Jump into experience while you are alive!
> Think . . . and think . . . while you are alive.
> What you call "salvation" belongs to the time before death.

The time is now, the elders advise. Even in moments of great suffering, the time is now to connect deeply to the experience of our very own lives. "A mountain worth climbing," I tell myself and my psychotherapy clients, knowing full well that it is a steep but invaluable climb.

In August 1992, I began a one-year internship in psychology on a pediatric oncology ward at The Dana-Farber Cancer Institute, one of the most highly regarded cancer treatment centers for children and adults in the world. During that year three other interns and I treated more than two hundred infants, children, and adolescents. We also counseled the families, as their daughters and sons struggled to recover from cancers and blood diseases. A few of our clients (as psychotherapy patients are known) were cured, most went into remission, and some died. It was a year of great suffering and of great giving, and it changed everything I understood about children and about life.

Imagine playing Candyland with a five-year-old facing amputation the next day. The child's face focuses on the draw: his eyes squint, his left hand fingers tap a rhythm, his head bends low to the board. This is the moment that concerns him—this card, this game, this win or loss. Cancer may be mutating his cells but what counts is that he is with someone he trusts, who is loving what he loves. This is his bottom line.

In the room next to him a teenager listens to REM while she awaits clearance for the next experimental round of drugs. She no longer plays games. Her worries are much more frightening, yet even she teaches that this day is all we have. When I approach her for therapeutic conversation she may or may not want to talk. At seventeen she has learned that her time is her own and some days it is far more useful to write letters to her girlfriends than to explore her anxiety about medication. "Chemo and girl talk don't mix," she tells me, so she writes to her friends about what color they should dye their hair on graduation day to freak out their parents. After four years battling lymphoma, she knows she must gather images of hope to give her the energy for the next day's cancer drama.

On the bone marrow ward, one girl is being sent home. Too sick for a transplant, she will die within days of leaving us. Her last gesture in the hospital is to give away something she loves to another child who still has a chance to live. It is hard to watch yet impossible to look away. How do we respond?

During my childhood, Highland Terrace, Gloversville, New York, marked the west side of the poor section of town. First- and second-generation immigrant families mingled with blue-collar mill workers, teachers, seamstresses, and laborers. We all knew each other's names, and the twenty-or-so kids on my block met daily at the top of our hill for kickball, spud, tag, and hide-and-seek. I had school buddies up and down the block, cousins living in the house behind ours, and my grandmother next door. Despite the fun and games, the everyone-looks-out-for-each-other feeling, and the safety of our sidewalks, from my earliest conscious memory, I was a worrier.

I memorized the faces of abducted children on milk cartons and would scan the lines at the A&P trying to find them. I saved pennies to send to starving children in Africa and India and prayed nightly for those who were sick. One afternoon, when I was eight, I gave away the hand-sewn, beaded Barbie dresses my grandmother had made for me to a girl with even less than we had. When my mother confronted me that night, I cried from frustration. I had no words to tell her that I felt I had to help.

Twenty years later, I volunteered at the New England Deaconess Hospital Mind/Body Clinic (now called the Mind/Body Medical Institute at Beth Israel Deaconess Hospital) before entering graduate school. At the Deaconess I learned that not everyone is cured through medicine alone—often the spirit, the heart, and sometimes the body are best served through a combination of support from the fields of psychology, medicine, and faith. I believed that somehow integrated disciplines could truly ease suffering, and in order to understand this concept more deeply, I entered graduate school in clinical psychology, studied the integration of psychotherapy and faith systems, and chose the med-psych pediatric oncology rotation at Dana-Farber for my last year of clinical training. I did not know how difficult the year would be for me personally, how it would strain my heart and my faith. I would leave the hospital a different woman than when I had entered.

Coming to know children in pain taught me the limits

of my profession and its usefulness—how psychology, through its adherence to language and conversation, offers only so much. It cannot prevent life's capricious touch, cure physical disease, or return a dead relative. And yet the act of listening to a person over time can bring about extraordinary changes for any human being, changes that can help a child love herself even as her body deteriorates or help an adult discover capacities for resilience, compassion, and joy.

My naïveté about the human spirit's capacity to handle anything was shattered at Dana-Farber and concomitantly my appreciation for what we are able to adjust to and give, even in the depths of suffering, grew exponentially. Time and again I saw the illness of a child break the heart of a parent or sibling, and even more often I witnessed those broken hearts open wide with a greater capacity to love.

Anyone who has ever spent time with a loved one who is ill comes to understand that the lines between medical science and the art of medical practice are blurred beyond recognition. My innocence about what medicine can and cannot do became transformed that year. I learned how physicians do what they can based on what they know, and what they don't know can be astonishing. Into that gap the good ones leap, using intuition, experimentation, and a willingness to go beyond the traditional borders of care to stretch the limits of the field. Through the creativity of these physicians, children lived who should not have, according to medical statistics, and some became fully cured despite obstacles others could not surmount. The term *miraculous* came to mind more than once that year at the hospital, as did a clear awareness that we don't yet fully know, either in psychology or medicine, what will definitively offer a cure for any one person.

Death, however, was the greatest new teacher. In any hospital, death is a part of the job. A beeper rings, the resident tells you your client, a nine-year-old, has died. As you hang up the phone images of the child rush forward in your mind and the beeper buzzes again and you are called to the clinic to greet a new client that moment. Life is present, always demanding your attention. You attend the funeral of a client and witness the family offering solace to others and you wonder, How is this possible; where does that strength come from? Or you meet with a boy who lost his sister, a boy who cannot yet understand death, and you ask yourself, How do any of us keep getting out of bed in the morning when suffering is omnipresent?

"I think this is the prettiest world—" Mary Oliver wrote in "The Kingfisher," "so long as you don't mind a little dying." And this is true and poignant. The wonder and the pain are inseparable and undeniable in a hospital—there is no escaping this reality.

For an inveterate worrier who wanted to make it all better, this was a reality nearly impossible to bear. But, over time I learned something remarkable. Thirteen years after Dana-Farber, it is those children and their stories that continue to bring the greatest richness. Because of them, of how they embraced their lives even in the face of pain, and of how they loved, even in dark moments, I have learned to live my life more fully and with greater care and gratitude.

A year in the presence of children dying, a lifetime of

caring for those with cancer and other diseases, with trauma and loss, and I find an urgency within me to discover beauty, wonder, and meaning where I can. I do not waste time on work or volunteer efforts that are uninspiring to me. I do not schedule my children into activities every afternoon. We search instead for the brook, the mountain, the playroom, the forest, and the bed we can all fit in—anyplace where connection to each other and to the larger world can happen without artifice.

The basics of self-care that I learned at the New England Deaconess Mind/Body Clinic—breathe, offer yourself quiet moments each day, name what you know, remember that I, you, all of us, are already unique and important—have become staples in my life. It was at the clinic that I received the first hint of knowing that pain can be addressed in nonmedical ways. When we treat ourselves with kindness, when we learn to physically relax our bodies and reduce both internal and external stressors, our experience of pain can change. By reducing the power of the negative forces that control our lives, they then consume less of our time and energy. When this happens we create room for positive energy to reenter, bringing with it all of life's beauty and wonder.

So, too, with grief. I now understand that grief, when accepted with self-compassion, can rise and fall and weave itself into the fabric of a life. Life will still blossom with what is new and compelling, even after loss, if we just choose to let it back in by opening our hearts.

Knowing that suffering is ever present and that life is inconstant, I urge my students, clients, everyone, to let go of the dross of their lives and instead spend their time ask-ing the deeper questions. These are the questions that heal us irrespective of what is happening in our lives. We do not need to be facing dire illness to know them and gain wisdom from them:

> Where are you safe?
> What is beautiful to you?
> What brings meaning to your life?
> Where do you find joy?
> What one step can you take to live a more authentic life?
> What makes you laugh?
> What are your dreams?
> Whom do you love?

And I also tell them the hair-dye story.

At the age of twenty-three my hair, a brown-black pile, began to go white. For years after, every time I would sit in a salon chair to get my hair cut, invariably I would be asked by the hairdresser, "So when are we going to do something about this gray?" I'd answer with anything I could think of: Hair dye is carcinogenic; I don't want to waste time coloring it every six weeks; I think it's beautiful the way it is; and so on. No answer was satisfactory to the stylist; beauty is so narrowly defined in our culture. One night in Boston I heard the poet David Whyte speak at a conference about the first moment of composing his poem, "Self-Portrait." Inspired by van Gogh's powerful self-portraits, Whyte looked into a mirror and expected to hear within himself a first line that in some way described his face. What came to him was a shock. He wrote, "It does not interest me if there is one god or many gods." Millions have died over this question, but it was not an issue meaningful to Whyte. He then spoke to us of the power of knowing the truth of one's life. I now had my answer. In the next stylist's chair, emboldened by the certainty that each day brings both suffering and the possibility of living life more fully, I turned as the stylist raised her eyebrows at my gray and deflected her before she could speak: "Hair color is not the question of my life."

When I began this book I was writing to honor a vow I had made to the children I treated, that their stories would not be forgotten. As their lives began to bloom again on the pages, I realized there was more here than a child's particular experience. Each story offered something true about living life while on the edge of death, and I understood, thirteen years postinternship, that I had been in the presence of great teachers. Their capacity to adapt, to give, to teach, and to create even while in pain astounds me now: That a child could be forced to swallow medications he detested one day and bring you his favorite toy to play with the next session. How a girl in the weeks before her leg amputation could challenge a therapist to hopping contests until it would "seem like [she] always never had two legs." How a teenager could sing as the needles came near and a little girl confidently describe the invisible shield the big pretty angel had sent to keep her safe.

To live in this world with an open heart, to witness

suffering and still get up each morning and make something out of one's day, isn't easy. The children I met faced these challenges every day that year, and for years to come. Their journeys were remarkable, for being so young when illness struck and for living through cancer without pretense or dishonesty. Their innocence, their joy, their vulnerability, their humor, and their courage—these were the gifts they left behind, and it is those very gifts that can help all of us live life awakened and open.

Many of my clients' stories are in the pages that follow. Each one is based directly on a child I treated. To preserve their privacy and protect the confidentiality of their treatment I have changed the details of their identities and their diseases—yet the emotion at the heart of each story is true. The hospital personnel are composite characterizations of many of the physicians and therapists and nurses I have worked with over the years at a number of hospitals. I hope my respect for them resonates throughout these pages.

May these children's lives offer you what they offered me—a certainty that wisdom can be attained whenever we choose to pay attention, that connection to each other matters deeply, that every life counts, and that we must love who we love while we can.

1
Part of a Life

Jake Weaver was five, a huge five, the kind of child a dad might proudly call "a bruiser." We met my first Friday on duty, three days into the training year, August 1992. A sweatpants-and-sweatshirt kid, he wore his buzz-cut brown hair under a camouflage fishing hat and carried a Teenage Mutant Ninja Turtles backpack jammed with action figures on his shoulder. In its outer zipper pouch, he stuffed a pale yellow blanket decorated with white ducklings and lambs, which, I would learn, he held during the worst exams.

Jake had ALL, acute lymphoblastic leukemia, not an uncommon cancer for a child of his age. His chemotherapy regimen required that he take pills for two weeks straight, have a week off, and begin the cycle again. He had responded well to the drugs during June and July, but now, in his tenth week, he refused to take any more pills. When faced with chemo pills at home, Jake fought hard and kept his mouth closed. In the last four days he had broken two water glasses, a breakfast bowl, one mirror, and a radio. His mom, Karen, had tried to muscle the pills

into her son with no success. Her husband, Scott, had re-
sorted to bribery and threats. Nothing worked. Jake was
serious; he was done with pills.

During the four days of Jake's tirade he had taken his
medicine one time out of eight. Karen had called Jake's
doctor that Friday morning, demanding a meeting of
Jake's team and a psychology consult. Two hours later I
met Jake.

Dana-Farber initially opened in 1947 as the Sidney Farber
Cancer Center in honor of its founding father, pathologist
Sidney Farber. It sits in the southwestern corner of Boston's
center of medical training sites and specialty hospitals.
Known for its brilliant medical minds and a history of
groundbreaking research in pediatric oncology, it practically
shimmered with scientific prestige. Research and training
dollars flowed in; new equipment, procedures, and protocols were available, often in the first or second rounds of
experimentation; and physicians from the top training
programs vied for the few spots open in any one year. Rumor had it that because of the hospital's prominence a
nurse or doctor would be hard-pressed to leave once he or
she was hired. The deeper reality was unspoken but understood: once hired, it was difficult to imagine working anyplace else; the hospital's reputation gave us all hope that
our work would be successful and a child's body could be
healed on any given day.

I was hired in August for a twelve-month psychology
rotation on the pediatric service along with three other

interns, Audrey, Paula, and Jason, a fourth-year psychology student and friend who was enrolled with me in a clinical psychology program. The psychology training suite on the hospital's fourth floor consisted of two adjoining rooms. Our supervisor, Donna Gentile, shared the smaller room with Sandra Brenton, a veteran of the department, who had worked in pediatric oncology for more than twenty years. The intern room was used for conferences, supervision sessions, and, most frequently, for play therapy with our clients. Workload was determined by one factor only: if you were at the hospital you were given the case. By the fourth week we each had a caseload of fifteen or more clients and were well aware that the previous year's interns finished their rotation with many more. Rotations through the pediatric clinic, where all children had to come for blood draws, physical exams, and chemo and radiation treatments, were decided by our academic schedules. Jason and I worked on Mondays and Thursdays. Audrey and Paula shared Tuesdays and Wednesdays, and we all worked on Fridays.

Fridays, we were warned that first week, were the most difficult days at the hospital. Parents worried that their children might decline over the weekends, so they became accustomed to bringing their sons and daughters in for last-minute checkups on Fridays. Statistics never supported this rumor, but the hospital norm was unshakable: if a parent wanted extra handholding on Friday we were told to provide it. As Donna said, "better an extra moment for no apparent reason on Friday, than a preventable emergency on Saturday." Jason, Audrey, Paula, and I complained during the first few weeks because Fridays were a nightmare as we juggled session time in the intern room.

By October our complaints had decreased. As our attachments to our clients deepened, so did our awareness that we would carry them with us over the weekend, no matter how healthy they had seemed on their last visit and no matter what medicines, practices, and prayers or incantations we had offered them. Bad things could happen when they were away from us. Seeing our clients on Fridays, as was the case that first day with Jake, gave us all—parents, therapists, nurses, and physicians—a sense of control.

I met Jake in examining room three. Wallpapered with dancing hippos, it contained a single bed, an IV pole, a standard hospital sink and cabinetry, one swivel stool, and an infant weighing scale. Dr. Mike Sontag, Jake's physician and chief resident, introduced me to Karen and Scott. Jake was in the clinic's waiting room, playing with his favorite nurse, Jill. I stood in the doorway in order to listen to the conversation while observing Jake. As a stranger to him, I wasn't certain I was going to be able to do much good this first meeting. Mike listened to Jake's parents recount his rebellion and concurred that this was serious. Jake couldn't afford to miss meds or be in charge of his own treatment. Mike asked me what I thought we should do. New to pediatric oncology and new to children as clients, I didn't have an answer. I stalled for time by asking Mike if he had ever seen this kind of behavior before.

"No," he said, "usually the kids are pretty compliant." This put the ball back in my court. Not wanting to let these parents down I suggested I page my supervisor. "She's been doing this for decades; let's see what she has to say."

I called Donna and to my surprise she was actually in her office. Briefing her over the phone at the clinic's desk I could see Jake lining up soldiers along the windowsill, explaining each one's magic powers to Jill. "This one shoots invisible laser bullets," he warned, holding a blue figure with an oversized gun in his hand. He was aiming the gun at the other children romping about in the playroom.

I moved behind the desk to keep the phone call private. I told Donna, "Mike wants this taken care of today. Jake's parents have tried the usual reward charts, threats, promises of gifts. None of it's worked. Any suggestions?"

Donna's answer was immediate and blunt. "Give him one choice, Maria. Tell him he has two minutes to take his pills right there in the office or he will be held down and forced to swallow."

"What? You want us to shove pills down his throat?" I asked. Jake had switched his attention to toy trucks, using a bulldozer to knock over enemy soldiers on the sill.

"Yes. Get everyone on the team involved except the parents. Let them be the good guys. But make sure Jake knows that they agree with the plan."

"Donna, he doesn't even know me. We have no alliance, and we don't even know why he's doing this." I watched as Jill helped Jake attack the enemy's hideout, a blue chair cushion under which Jake had hidden dinosaurs and an alien. They sneaked around to the back of the chair, Jake attacking from overhead as Jill lifted the pillow with an "ah hah!"

"Maria, you don't have time for an alliance. He has to understand now that he has no other option. As for why he's doing it, it's pretty simple. He either hates it, is afraid of it, or is too overwhelmed to care. His internal process is not as important in this moment as his chance to stay alive. You could do weeks of puppet play about this and still not know what is going on in a five-year-old's head. He doesn't have weeks."

"This is going to be hard."

"Keep it quick. Tell him once, give him the time limit, then have the team hold him down; you are not to be part of the physical restraint. You don't want his anxiety to build any more than it has to. Tell him you will do this each time he has to take meds until he does it himself at home. One more thing. It's okay that it's hard. Just think of how hard cancer is for a child."

I hung up, stunned.

Dr. Mike and Jake's parents agreed with the plan without question. The parents had already had to make harsh choices: to keep Jake away from his friends and school to reduce the risk of infection, to change work so that some-one would be home with Jake every hour each day, to drive for hours each visit to provide him with care at this hospital, instead of in their local hospital. They were relieved to have a plan.

After I took Jill aside and explained what we were going to do, she brought Jake into the examining room and invited two of the male nurses, Bill and Rich, in as well. We put Jake on the bed and I introduced myself.

"Jake, we don't know each other. My name is Maria, and I'm going to be a part of your team. Dr. Mike asked me to help make sure you take your meds. We understand from your parents that you haven't taken them lately. Is that right?"

Jake kept his head down and fiddled with his knees.

"So we don't really have many options because you need the medicine to make you better." I waited for a response, but Jake remained silent.

"Here's the deal then. I'm going to ask Jill to get the egg timer from the treatment room. We're going to set it for two minutes. You have those two minutes to take the pills yourself, just like you used to do at home. If you choose not to take them, then we'll have to hold you down and make you take them."

Jake glowered at me, got off the bed, and walked over to his dad. Scott said nothing, but picked his son up.

"We don't want to force you to take these pills, Jake," I continued, "but nothing is more important than getting the cancer out of you, and we need to have the medicine inside you to do that. Do you understand the deal?"

Jake pulled his dad's head down and whispered to him.

Scott shook his head. "There's no going home until you take the pills, Jake."

At that Jill got the egg timer, and Mike placed the pills on a tray on the bed. I could smell my own sweat. Scott put Jake on his lap on the bed. I put the tray on Jake's lap, and said, "Okay Jake, it's up to you. You have two minutes to take your pills."

The previous day, in six minutes time, I had seen an oncologist palpate a girl's spine, mark a tiny circle, prep the skin with betadine, place a sterile paper drape with a four-inch hole centered over the circular mark, inject lidocaine to anesthetize the skin, slip a needle into the canal and administer chemo into the spinal fluid to inhibit leukemic cells from going to the brain, hand the syringe over to the waiting nurse, reassure the girl, remove his gloves, pat her head, wink at the parent holding her daughter's hand, and leave. That time is not wasted in a hospital was obvious to me prior to my internship. What I learned in the first week of my rotation was that time was a certain enemy. Like the sudden-death period in a hockey match, every second counted. The disease, it seemed, controlled the clock and would not hesitate to end the game precipitously.

The timer was running. Jake turned once to his mom, who smiled through her tears and told him that she knew he could do this. He stared at the pills and for the full two minutes did nothing. No words, no fighting, no sighing, no kicking; he simply sat and let the egg timer tick away. At one minute and forty seconds, I had signaled his mom to move out of the way. Jake sat still. At one minute fifty I'd sent Mike to the head of the bed, the two male nurses to the sides, and positioned myself at the foot. I let Jill decide where she wanted to be.

When the egg timer rang, Jake jumped in his dad's lap, causing the pills to fall. I gathered them quickly saying, "Scott, please move to the door." Jake went to move with him, and I picked up this fierce, unknown boy and put him back on the bed. As I tried to lay him down, he kicked me in the neck. Mike immediately grabbed his shoulders and Bill and Rich reached to restrain his arms. Jake was struggling hard now. I went to hold his feet and remembered Donna's last-minute advice. I was not to actually be involved in the restraint. I backed off and stood instead near his knees. Jill had gone to Jake's right side and was trying to soothe him. I couldn't hear what she was saying; it took all my attention to keep myself steady.

"Jake," Mike warned, "you have to do this, buddy. We're going to be here as long as it takes. You have to do this."

The child fought, screaming and writhing, shouting for his parents to help him. His mom cried openly. Scott pressed his hands on my back, willing me to end this. I leaned forward so Jake could hear me and told him we were going to put a pill in his mouth. I signaled Mike. He held Jake's head in one arm and slipped one pill in against his cheek. Jake began to gag on the pill, and Mike lifted his head to help him swallow. Jill offered water, but Jake began shaking his head and moaning, "No, no, no, no," over and over.

"Mike, did he swallow it?" I had to shout over Jake's moans.

"I don't know. Jake, is it down?"

Jake spat the pill out at Jill, and I took it and put it back in Mike's hand. Mike opened Jake's jaw and slid the pill in, telling Jake we wouldn't give up. Jill was crying now. She pleaded with Jake to swallow. Mike's face was inches from Jake's, and he kept repeating, "It will be okay, it will be okay. You have to have the pills to make it okay." Jake's moaning quieted. He tried to sit up straight. I told him he couldn't come off the bed until all the pills were inside him. He opened his mouth to show me that the pill was gone. I signaled Mike for the next pill.

"Good job. Which one do you want next?" I was desperate to give him control over his own body. My hands trembled; I tried to hide my nervousness from him.

He looked at me mutely and I chose for him. "Jake, I'm going to give you this one next. If you want a different one, pick it now." I showed Jake a pill. He didn't move. I handed it to Mike, and he put it in Jake's mouth. This time Jake turned to Jill for water. He took the last pill soundlessly, his arms slack, his face down toward his chest. I could hear others sobbing but couldn't turn my attention away from Jake. Mucus collected in my nose and throat, tears threatening to come. There was something even more painful in his resignation than in his fighting—to break a child's spirit is a brutal act.

Bill, Rich, and I moved away from the bed to let his parents comfort him. Mike stepped back into the doorway, holding onto the lintel. Karen climbed onto the bed and gathered Jake into her arms, while Scott rubbed his back. In his mother's embrace, Jake sobbed openly. We were quiet, letting him find his way back to safety. When a few moments had passed I spoke.

"Jake, we are so proud of you, so proud." He burrowed his head into Karen.

"You're so strong," Jill cheered. "We needed four people to hold you down."

Mike chimed in, "You're the strongest kid I know, Jake." At that Jake smiled, lifting his head to look at Mike, two brown eyes cresting just above his mother's shoulder.

"Your strength is going to help you beat the bad guys," I added. "But you need extra power, just like your ninja guys, to win against the aliens. The pills are your extra power, and we aren't going to let you fight this cancer without them."

Jake didn't turn his face or meet my eyes. Who knew if my words had much impact on him, given what he had just experienced? Without a relationship, they were at best a shot in the dark. I asked Karen when he had to take his medicine again.

"After supper," she answered.

Scott picked his son up out of Karen's arms. Jake let his dad hold him for a moment, then scrambled to the ground. I knelt to speak with him face-to-face.

"Jake, Dr. Mike and the nurses are going to have to leave. I'll stay here with you and your parents and we can talk about whether you are going to take the pills at home like you used to or if you need us to help you take them again tonight." He spun away immediately and stuck his head between his father's knees.

Mike and Bill and Rich left, each giving Jake a pat on

the back. Jill gave Jake a hug, repeating how proud she was of him and asking him to find her again before he left. Alone with him and his parents, I told Karen and Scott how sorry I was that we had had to do this to their son, that they were all unusually brave, and that I knew how it must have hurt them to witness his struggle. I treated Jake as if he were a much older child, writing my pager number in large print on a piece of paper and handing it to him. I explained to Jake that he needed to call me when he had made up his mind about taking the next round of medicine. Then I suggested that they might want some private time now. Ten paces down the hallway as I turned the corner I heard Scott calling my name. Jake had given them his answer.

"What do you think, Jake?" I asked as I walked back to the treatment room.

"I'll take the pills by myself," he said softly.

"That's great. C'mon, let's go tell Jill and Dr. Mike." I gave him a big thumbs up.

As I walked back to the intern office the August sun shone through the glass hallways, late summer heat that seared. My eyes had trouble focusing. Was it all going to be this intense?

I rested my forehead against the window and tried to breathe slowly. Clinicians, nurses, and secretaries walked by me as if I weren't there. The glass warmed the center of my forehead, as my head and body shook from pressure and fear. My childhood had been bracketed by the loss of two men I adored: my grandfather Joseph Sirois, dead of multiple myeloma when I turned three, and a twenty-seven-year-old cousin, Tommy Johnson, lost to a brain tumor my sophomore year in college. Now I knew someone else with cancer.

Breathing into the sunlight might not be enough.

On Monday, Jake returned for his regular checkup. He brought his superhero collection for us to play with and offered me the first pick. We were to surround the enemy (a stuffed twelve-inch-tall dinosaur) and attack simultaneously. He told me exactly where to hide my hero, when to engage, and when I'd have to take cover. Lying on the floor of the psychology intern room, I was happy and surprised. I had expected us to have to warm up to each other slowly given Friday's traumatic encounter. But Jake had his own priorities: play came first, cancer second. He understood the drill now, Karen would tell me at the end of the session. As long as Jake took his pills, his days could be full of the things he loved.

We did not have to hold Jake down again. For the length of that year, he was a compliant, loving child, who brought his toys to each session and asked only that we play together. Over time, Jake, his parents, and I became connected, and we learned as a group what Jake needed to know before each treatment or test: that he was loved, that he could play with the things he loved, and that he would not ever go through this alone.

At the end of the year, Jake brought me a handmade birdhouse, rough pieces of misaligned wood painted in the palette of childhood—sky blue, sunflower orange, neon green, lemon yellow. It was small enough for me to hold in one hand. He cradled the birdhouse against his chest, an offering of great pride. As he held it out to me, he ducked his head in a shy smile. Karen spoke for him, telling me that he and his father had crafted the house and Jake had selected the wood, the colors, and the shape. Jake had told her on the way over that he hoped I would hang it someplace where I could see it daily and be reminded of him. He wanted to say thanks for the good times we had had.

I had no words with which to respond, other than to offer a thank-you that was filled with wonder. Jake and I smiled at each other for a long moment, then gave each other a long good-bye hug.

Placing the birdhouse on my kitchen windowsill that evening I shook my head. How was it possible that this year meant good times to him? His chart was full of notes that marked a year of difficulty: vomiting; bed-wetting; anger at having to miss his friends' parties, school events, and vacation; worry that his parents would not love him if he didn't get better; mood swings; insomnia; nighttime fears. This would have been enough for me to have considered it a bad year, a very bad year.

With time, I understood something: Jake's youth and innocence supplied him with a protection and a knowledge I had forgotten. If you can live in the moment doing what you love, as children can, and you are surrounded by those you trust, then suffering is ameliorated and it becomes a part, not the whole, of your life.

2
Do No Harm

By October 1, four weeks into our year, we interns had absorbed one truth at the hospital: there is little we carry that can heal terror. As novice therapists we tended to gather as many objects and techniques as we could to offer to our clients—like new parents buying toys, hoping to make their children happy. Our consultation room was a jumble of stuff. Two shelves housed games: checkers, chess, Candyland, Sorry, Chutes and Ladders, pickup sticks, marbles, Yatzee, memory games, and playing cards. A toy box was filled with hand puppets, finger puppets, dress-up clothes, stuffed animals, and soft balls. Picture books were scattered throughout the room.

Some books offered illustrations done by children of themselves without hair, without limbs, or lying in hospital beds with big printed block letters saying CANCER HURTS, or IT'S OKAY TO CRY. Three plastic doctor kits sat above Jason's desk beside a doll with detachable limbs and hair, and an eighteen-inch-high figurine with removable organs. The fake syringes and bandaids had to be replaced often. Most children were fascinated by playing doctor, repeating the procedures done to them over and over, now as the person in power.

Through the years, interns added to the collection. Jason brought Matchbox cars. I kept a smiling lion, two Christmas teddy bears, and face paint on my desk. Audrey filled a drawer with play makeup and mirrors, barrettes, and hair ribbons, and Paula contributed coloring books, pencils, and crayons. Absent from the room were war toys. Soldiers, Indians and cowboys, knights and dragons, guns, arrows, and games like Battleship and Stratego were unwelcome. It was difficult enough to live with the aggression visited upon the children's bodies in the hospital; we needed no other evidence of violence.

Yet sometimes a child demanded war. Jake and I constructed paper swords and lined up the dolls and animals for enemy attack. Or we'd prepare for alien invasion, shielding our bodies with imaginary domes designed to ward off lasers, bullets, and arrows. Often we, the good guys, would win and escape into protected territory where the aliens could not enter. But sometimes, when Jake's terror was close at hand, we would be defeated, our imaginary blood leaking onto the carpet as victorious enemies held spears to our throats. I would ask, "What do we do now?" to determine how he might find his way to safety.

But it wouldn't be the objects or games, our supervisors advised us, that would make a difference. It would be our ability to relate to the child and his or her ability to connect with us that would matter.

We quickly learned that each child required a unique relationship. Some thrived with imaginary play, some with direct conversation; others worked through emotion on the game board, in competition. One child, an eight-year-old with white-blond hair and a strawberry mole under her right eye, chose to speak through her diary. Our sessions consisted of parallel letter writing and sharing. Once we drew pictures together on a chalkboard of what she might look like posttransplant. I drew a child, thin and bald, but seated upright with eyes open. She drew herself as a five-year-old, three years younger than her age, ready to play kickball with a sibling. When I attempted to discuss her imagery, she erased our drawings; words can be too much in the moment.

To help with our clients' pain, we interns had training sessions each week. We were taught hypnotherapy, biofeedback, guided imagery, and cognitive restructuring. In-service lectures were given on the use of humor, puppet play, art therapy, and meditation. To these we added our particular theoretical orientation and beliefs about how a person remains resilient in trauma's wake. We absorbed articles defining the effectiveness of psychotherapy; was it the relationship between therapist and client that helped, the therapist's interventions, specific techniques, the presence of a caring listener? What was it, we asked each other, that most enabled a child to endure cancer and reaffirmed his or her strengths?

For our inpatients, those children too sick to be treated in the clinic or those facing surgery, transplant, and amputations, these questions became even more complicated. Sessions were compromised by medical interruptions, basic needs such as sleep or private time, and reactions to surgeries and transplants: infection, fever, vomiting, diarrhea, skin rashes, mouth sores, liver toxicity, and falling blood levels. We adjusted our work accordingly, meeting the children for brief visits, calling often, leaving notes, returning at night when it seemed necessary and appropriate.

The medicines themselves were often problematic, exacerbating suffering. Drugs intended to cure brought ruin to immune and digestive systems, sleep patterns, sensory awareness, mobility, and in some cases, fertility. The concomitant psychological onslaught could be profound. Anxiety and panic, depression, even paranoia appeared when pain or fear pressed too close. Cancer heightened any vulnerability a child had, causing some children to regress to an early stage of development. Ten-year-olds would take to sleeping with their parents or begin bed-wetting. Five-year-olds would have nightmares each time they rested. One twelve-year-old began to suck her thumb whenever she smelled the antiseptic cleanser used at the hospital. Regression often revealed shame and a hidden worry that cancer had come because the child was unworthy or unwanted.

In a parallel experience, we interns worried that we would not get it right or might in some way damage a child's psyche. It was a concern that made us determined to learn all we could immediately. We found ourselves studying case histories and medical texts and grilling former interns to find that one technique that would move a child toward greater peace, acceptance, tolerance, or fearlessness. We dreamed about our kids, called each other frequently, and began to practice pain management techniques on our colleagues and friends.

Four weeks into the rotation our clients had become more than just names and faces. They each had their own story, which made the statistics we were given even more frightening. In that year alone, 1993, the American Cancer Society predicted that 15 out of every 100,000 children would get cancer and 3.7 out of every 100,000 would die. More than a decade later, the numbers are still forbidding: In 2004, over 9,200 children between the ages of zero and fourteen were diagnosed with cancer (still about 15 out of every 100,000) and in this age group alone an estimated 1,510 deaths occurred in the United States (approximately 3.2 out of every 100,000). Forty-six children a day under the age of fifteen are diagnosed each year, and while mortality rates have decreased steadily since 1975, cancer was and is the primary cause of death by disease for children in this age group.

In those early days on the ward it wasn't clear what exactly would help any one child. If it wasn't the toys, games, and puppets and if therapeutic conversation could be easily derailed by medical needs, then how could we make a positive difference? We were not sure. We knew only this for certain: none of us wanted to cause harm when harm was already being done in the service of cure.

3
All Clear

"Shit," I said, slamming my hockey stick against my shin. I had lost the ball for the second time to my opponent, a blonde giant with speed. I had been lightning fast in my twenties, but at thirty-one I was definitely beatable. "Damn," I swore again, upset with myself that my age had cost us another chance to score. It was us old folks from the regional postcollege traveling league against the local college varsity field hockey squad. It was a matter of great pride that our old-lady team, many of us champions in our day, had beaten the varsity a number of times in the last seven years. It was practically unheard of in the annals of hockey history. The varsity players were always younger, better trained, better equipped, and in better shape. Something about our core group still worked though. We were wiser about how to use our energy, not afraid to try new moves, and most of us, myself included, had played hockey since eighth grade, so few plays from our opponents could surprise us.

With the score now tied two to two, I had to think. My nemesis, Jules, was standing next to me. We were waiting for the "all clear" from the referee. She had awarded the ball to the varsity, and the fullback was lining up to strike it out of her goal zone into midfield. If I could get to the hit first, I was extremely close to the goal and might have a good shot. I needed a plan. A close-in scramble would not work with Jules—she could muscle me out easily. I looked around. My teammates stared at the ball. I didn't want to lose.

The referee was replacing divots. I had a minute. Instinct took over. I began to do something I had done as a kid, which annoyed the hell out of my brothers. Like an eight-year-old, I played copycat. I scrunched my left sock down and threw out the shin pad, exactly as Jules had done minutes earlier. I placed my hands on my stick where Jules held hers, cocked my head at the same angle, and leaned left as she did. She was looking at me now, not happy. I had her attention. Good. I went further. My shirttail came out, I moved my lip out and eyebrows up, a clear imitation of her stare. "What the hell?" she blurted.

"What's up, Barbie?" I replied, and at that second the referee signaled the all clear, the ball was struck, and I was off with Jules left standing, caught in a childhood gambit. I reached the ball and struck left across the circle, a clean pass to my forward, Jan. She lifted the ball back to me at the post, a perfect arc to the right, sending the goalie into a spin. I raced in, batted the ball back and down to the opposite post. Score. Awesome. We held them for the remaining twelve minutes. Final score three to two. We had done it again. I was beyond psyched. My teammates hoisted me into the stands, where the rest of my team were jumping up and down and shrieking. Our coaches broke out the beer and soda and we toasted ourselves, old ladies all.

Two hours later, I drove home, rocking to Melissa Etheridge, screaming out my open window, "Somebody bring me some water." I was cool, I was victorious, I won the game. I walked in the house, ripped my sweatshirt off, and pranced around, yelling through the kitchen, "I am home, I am a Goddess." Within seconds the phone rang. I froze. Donna's voice on my answering machine was warm but brusque. "Maria, call me as soon as you get this. It's about Lily, important, but not urgent."

I slumped into the kitchen chair and took a few minutes to readjust. Hockey was a great release for me on Sundays, but the pager was never turned off and I had to be on call 24/7 that year. Donna and I covered for each other on the weekends so that I could attend my hockey games and she her painting classes.

I rolled my socks down and unlaced my cleats one hole at a time, stuffing paper towels in them to dry them out. I dialed Donna's number. "Hey, Donna, thanks for covering. What's up with Lily?"

"She's going home tomorrow, Maria. She'd like to see you in the morning, and you should spend time with her mom and dad as well. You'll need to prepare them for the next few weeks."

"Paul called you?" I asked. Paul Movson was Lily's doctor, one of the residents on the floor.

"This morning. He made the call to send her home and set up hospice care for them to start tomorrow night. He'll be around tomorrow to say good-bye as well." For the next twenty minutes, we discussed how best to prepare Lily for her trip home. From the beginning of that year I had noticed that no one on the psychology staff engaged in small talk, but we all gave each other hours of support about our clients. I hung up the phone and sat there, tracing the sweat stains on my legs. I had played hockey for seventeen years, the length of Lily's life.

Soft carpeting and comfortable chairs gave the hospital's lobby a welcoming aura. Security officers and information-desk staff were available as soon as a patient entered through its glass double doors. Elevators, off to the left of the lobby, opened and closed with soft dings, and to the right was a simple, small chapel and a gift shop. In the center of the space, a large circular staircase brought staff and families to and from the cafeteria. Despite heavy traffic, conversations were muted in this elegant lobby; it projected a feeling of stability and care, for not one detail appeared to have been hastily considered.

Lily's mom, Celia, came through the lobby alone. Dressed in slacks, sneakers, and a sweater set, her characteristic book bag was not on her arm. Celia was famous in the hospital for bringing the latest Parent's Choice Award books for Lily to read to the younger children. Together, Celia and Lily had spent hours in the pediatric oncology playroom, reading the classics—*Charlotte's Web*, *Winnie the Pooh*, *Where the Wild Things Are*, and *Thomas the Tank Engine*—to the three- and four-year-olds. When Lily had become nearly blind a few months earlier, Celia had kept up the ritual, sharing her time between Lily's bedside and reading to the little ones.

Following my conversation with Donna the night before, I had called Celia and we decided to meet the next day in the lobby before going to Lily's room. Confidentiality had long since stopped being an issue for this family. Lily had been treated here since she was nine; it was more comfortable for them to be known and greeted by staff walking by than to be hidden in an office somewhere.

"Hi, Celia. Barry's not here?" I took the chair next to her, noting the absence of Lily's father.

"He's staying with her. The team has a lot of information to give us. I'm too tired to listen." Celia offered a half smile and then dropped her head and picked at her sweater with one hand.

"The air-conditioning is cold today," she continued.

"Is Lily cold? I'll see if we can change it."

"No, it's alright, we'll be gone soon." At that she looked up again, eyes wet and hands still.

"I spoke with Donna last night and she told me Paul's decision."

"She's been here eight years. She knows this place better than her own neighborhood."

I nodded, my image of the hospital changing suddenly to that of a small city where travelers take up residence but never feel at home.

I motioned toward the elevator that would take us to Lily's room. "Is there anything specific you want me to discuss with Lily, anything you are concerned about for her today?"

Celia began crying, tears spotting her navy pants, the way the first drops of rain spot a driveway. We watched the tears settle together. After a time Celia shook her head.

"She trusts you," she said. "Just tell her what you think is best."

"Okay then." I stood up. "I'll talk to you after our session."

Celia squeezed my hand, indicating that she wanted one more moment. I followed her gaze to the lobby's main door, opening and closing with each entrant.

"I'm a little relieved. Is that okay? Yesterday, when we talked to Paul, I felt this whoosh in my legs, and I realized that I was going to faint, so I sat down. I felt dizzy, but it wasn't because I was sad. I was glad to have it finally be over. She has suffered here for so long that, well, I don't want her to die, I don't want to lose my baby, but it's been so long. Am I awful?"

I wanted to take her in my arms, this mother of seven who was feeling guilty at the thought that her middle daughter's suffering would end soon.

"You are not awful. There is nothing wrong with any of your feelings. Anyone in your place would feel this way."

She bowed her head again, covering her face with her hands. I remember hearing the toilet flush and the noise of the cafeteria workers cleaning breakfast trays below. The hospital doors continued to swing open. I watched an elderly man wheel an elderly woman in behind a well-dressed woman wearing a head scarf. A family stood at the reception desk—parents, two boys, and a small girl. The receptionist pointed toward the elevator bank.

I waited for Celia's weeping to subside, remaining near enough so she could feel the warmth of my body. In the space of the next three minutes I watched perhaps nineteen people come and go. Families assembled and disassembled like a living kaleidoscope in front of the lobby desk and the elevator banks; the door never closed for more than twenty seconds that morning. Words from a psychology instructor played through my mind: It is all a matter of holding on or letting go. Life can be reduced in most moments to this—the struggle to hold on and to let go.

I had met Lily in August, at the end of her treatment for medullo blastoma, a brain and spinal cord cancer. For eight years the "best of the pediatric best" had tried everything, from an appropriate cancer protocol, to a few things that were strictly from the realm of we'll-do-whatever-it-takes-to-keep-her-alive. Lily's cancer would disappear for months at a time, only to reappear in tiny spots she called motes. "It's like the dust motes in the light, Maria. You can't see them unless you really look for them and the light is just right, but they're there all the time, even when you aren't looking," she explained to me on my first visit.

Cancer hit when Lily had just begun to find her own way. A middle child, with an older sister, two older brothers, and three younger sisters, Lily Sand was the student in the family. The elder Sand children had made their marks in athletics and the younger ones were a mixed bag of clowns and actors, but Lily, according to Barry and Celia, was the smart one, the thoughtful one. A few months before her diagnosis Lily had won a regional contest for her essay "The Beauty of the American People." Her premise had been that Americans were special because they took care of people in many nations. In one of our talks I suggested that she saw in America something that was fully present in herself, compassion. Lily thought about that for a day or two, then asked me if I thought we see in others what we have inside us, or what we wish we had more of inside us.

Celia and I took the elevator to Lily's room. We entered together, then Celia signaled Lily's father to leave with her. I stood at Lily's side and touched her hand. She had been a thin child, but years of high-dose steroids and chemo had caused her to gain weight. Her face was round and yellow-white, and her brown hair was scattered over her scalp in patches. She had lost most of her sight and her speech had become slow. In the past two weeks, she had regressed rapidly. Lily had always preferred conversation or being read to to game playing, but when her last treatment (pinpoint, high-dose radiation to the brain called stereotactic radio-surgery) had failed fifteen days earlier, she had asked to have her childhood toys brought to her. Our sessions were spent discussing what she could remember about playing with her dolls and stuffed animals. She enjoyed having me hold them and guess their names and would ask me to determine which had been her favorites.

Standing near her bed, I saw that her things had been packed, except for a stuffed Dalmatian puppy, Spots, that she had had with her since her third Christmas.

"Hey, Lily. It's me. You are heading home today."

"Can you sit with me now?"

"I can stay as long as you like, honey." I pulled a chair up next to her bed. She put out her hand for a moment, then settled it back under the covers. All I could see above the blanket was her face.

"What do you think it will be like for you at home, Lily?"

"Noisy."

I laughed. "I bet it never gets quiet with all those brothers and sisters."

"Mom says they're all coming home tonight. I'm going to have my favorite dinner."

"Wait, let me guess. Blueberry pie, mashed potatoes, no vegetables, and steak."

"No, that's your favorite. Remember? I like spaghetti and garlic bread, and strawberries on vanilla ice cream."

"Right."

"I can have whatever I want now, but I don't feel so hungry."

"I know, sweetie." We let silence hold us for a moment. Outside the door her parents waited, counting down their daughter's remaining time. We could hear the room's ventilation unit hum and the phone ring in the adjacent room.

"How does it feel not to have any IVs in?" I asked.

"Good, I guess. I don't really feel it so much anymore."

"Lily?"

"Yeah?"

I softened my voice. "Is there anything you want to ask about going home or saying good-bye, or dying?"

"I wish I could see Amanda play soccer." Her eyebrows had lifted at her own thought.

"Amanda's the superstar forward, right?"

"Yeah, I'm not gonna go to college. I wish I could see her play."

"I'm sorry, Lily. That isn't going to happen."

"I know." She shut her eyes.

I could hear a nurse's rubber clogs squeaking on the floor, getting louder, and then stopping in front of Lily's door. Voices murmured softly; everyone on the floor would want to say good-bye to this family.

"I just want to make it to my mom's birthday."

"When is that?"

"In three weeks, just before Thanksgiving."

"What did Dr. Paul say?"

"He said that it could happen." I gave a silent cheer for Paul's graciousness.

"Maybe you could tell your sisters and brothers what you want to do for your mom's birthday. That way, if you aren't feeling up to it, they could get it ready for you."

"Yeah, I like that idea. It'll be like a project to do."

The door opened then and Paul walked in. He cleared his throat to signal to Lily and spoke without checking to see if it was a good time. In oncology, there is only the present time for physicians. The pressure of a full schedule, unexpected emergencies, interns and residents to train, exhaustion from being on call, and the relentless pager all cohere to create a hospital environment where doctors often do not wait for a better moment—later may not arrive for myriad reasons both practical and awful.

"Lily, you're all cleared to go. Your parents have what they need to take care of you at home. The hospice nurse will be there soon after you arrive." I noticed that Lily had turned her face away, toward the window. Paul noticed, too, and lowered his voice. "We'll miss you, Lily." Both hands clutched the ends of his stethoscope as he waited for her response. He folded the scope carefully, tucked it into his coat pocket, and stepped toward her. "I'll go talk to your parents now and say good-bye to them." Lily didn't respond. His shoulders shrugged. I could see the corners of his mouth twitching down while his lips pursed outward, yet no further words came. "The doctor to man stumbles," writes Richard Selzer in *Mortal Lessons*, "most often wounds; his patients die, as must he." Paul looked around the room, turned quickly, and shut the door firmly behind him. All clear to go.

Lily hadn't moved even at the sound of the closing door. For a second I panicked, thinking I couldn't hear her breathing. I touched her shoulder, ashamed of my own fear. She shook her head with the slightest movement.

"Maria, I don't want to talk anymore."

"Okay, honey, I'll say good-bye then. I'll call you at home tomorrow, and we can talk then if you'd like."

"Can you call me every day?" she asked.

"Every day."

"Okay."

"Bye, sweetie." I reached up to stroke her head, allowing myself to feel her skull for just a second, and held myself back from kissing her. The boundaries of psychology mandate extreme care in having physical contact with a client, and the norm is clear—do not touch. I found it impossible to leave without that one gesture of connection and worried about it for days afterward. Is it okay to touch the head of a child who is leaving to die? Would it have been cruel not to?

I stepped back, taking in her shape. Its roundness and paleness reminded me of something not quite yet born. I said one more good-bye and left.

That night I dreamed of children skiing, learning the basic ski positions, french-fry and pizza-pie, as they tumbled and rode small hills decorated in white sequins and pearls. I had come to photograph them for a newspaper, and at the end of their lesson, I had them gather at the base of one of the hills and stand, shoulder to shoulder in one line. They stood restlessly, some laughing, others tickling their neighbors. Two boys peed designs on the snow. The line reached around the hill. I knew I would have to find a different camera, one that could see through the hill to the children on the other side. As I dug through my bag to find the new equipment, I asked the children to take their helmets off. I stood with the seeing camera, a cone-shaped telescope with a sight glass encircled in steel on top. I lifted the camera to my eye, looked through the lens, and saw on each head a baldness that blinded, reflecting light streams up to the sun. I attempted to focus the camera again and again, but it could not find its view through the luminosity and I gave up, disappointed to have nothing to show the children. I bent to gather their helmets, aware that I would have to make many trips.

4
Novitiate

"What are you doing? It's only two." Jason had walked by the clinic room to see me heading out on an early November Thursday, a day we both typically stayed until five.

"I screwed up. I need a break. Donna's going to cover for a few minutes; I'll be back later."

"Who'd you screw up with?" Jason threw his coat on the back of the chair.

"A new kid, no one you know, and I'm not staying to talk." I was at the door.

"Bad?"

"I didn't kill anybody, if that's what you mean." He walked me down the hall.

"Hey, aren't you being hard on yourself?" Jason grabbed me at the stairwell door.

"Not sure yet. I'll work that out with my own shrink. Bye." I slammed the door and ran down the four flights and out onto the street.

* * *

"Blood-draw day for Brian Morris. Who's up?" Roberta, head nurse at the clinic, had paged me that morning for help with a difficult draw. I had come down to the clinic to find the nurses gathered near the supply room arguing about whose turn it would be to take blood from a boy.

"Not me, I got him last time." Sandy crossed her arms.

"That's mature of you," countered Bill.

"When's the last time you were up, mister?" Sandy poked Bill in the chest with her finger.

"I'm out. He doesn't even know me." Rich leaned back, putting his hands behind his head.

"I'm here to help, if that helps," I offered. The team laughed.

"You must be the fourth or fifth shrink to try. Ain't no use, lady. Brian doesn't chill for anyone," said Sarika, the clinic receptionist. Clearly, taking Brian's blood was an event.

"Who's the best draw?" I needed to end this quickly; I had too many clients to spend the morning with nurses fighting over who had to draw blood from one child.

"Sandy," everyone except Sandy chorused.

"Alright, Sandy. It's you and me. Tell me what hasn't worked before."

For fifteen minutes I was treated to the two-year history of Brian Morris and his blood-draw shenanigans. Eleven-year-old Brian was in remission for Ewing's sarcoma and doing nicely. He had responded to chemo quickly and returned to school within days of treatment. His Hickman porta-cath, also known as a central line, had enabled him to get medicines and have blood drawn without needles while he had been receiving ongoing treatment. But the porta-cath had long since been removed, which presented a problem since blood still needed to be drawn monthly. Brian cooperated well except when it came time to use needles. He detested blood; the sight of it made him nauseous, histrionic, and belligerent. Faced with a needle, the staff had had to hold him down, a difficult event due to his size—he weighed nearly 110 pounds—and his spirit. Brian would shriek, scream, yell, and curse at each attempt. Often the needles were dislodged from the nurses' hands, and other children in the clinic panicked at his reaction. His draws were now done in a private room with only one nurse. His team had hoped—to no avail—that the reduced stimulation would help calm him.

Complicating each draw were his parents. They refused to participate, adamant that they not be put in the position of "bad guys," and they demanded that he not be given sedatives. They did not want Brian "overmedicated." Each month staff members fought to not be the one to have to do his blood draw; the loser often had to spend up to two hours trying to get one successful stick.

"What have other psychologists tried?" I asked while Sandy and I were alone in an examination room, waiting for Brian.

"I know the last one tried meditation and hypnotherapy, but that didn't work."

"How about Donna? Has she ever been called in?"

"Yeah, early on she tried some sort of psychodrama. But that was a disaster." Sandy had prepared the tray. The three vials and a syringe sat at the far end of the counter, under a white cloth. "She keeps asking the parents to consider anxiety meds, but they won't budge."

"Have you brought his doc in?"

"They don't have time to manage this. Sometimes they'll come in for five minutes or so."

"So how do you get it done?"

"We usually just struggle with him, until he's worn out. It takes about two hours. It's exhausting."

Rich poked his head in. "Brian spotted in the lobby. You've got three minutes. What are you gonna try?"

"None of your business," I said. His smirk was just a little too much like that of an older brother's.

I walked to the window and thought for a moment. This boy's energy reminded me of Jake's, and I knew the same principle should apply here—keep the event as brief as possible to limit Brian's anxiety. One other thought came to mind. In hypnosis, two contrary positions seemed to help: to distract from the fear so that it ceases to exist in the moment, or to name the fear so concretely that it becomes known, almost familiar. Paradoxically, looking closely at terror's face often frees a child from his fear. Something about this idea felt promising, but I didn't have time to think further because Brian's father, Jordan, knocked at the door.

We said to come in and he pushed Brian into the room. "Oh, hi, Sandy. Here's Brian. We've already checked in at the desk. Mike will see him when you are through. Be a good kid, Brian; I'll see you when it's over." He dashed out before I could even see his face. Brian was standing in the corner near the door, staring at the covered tray. Dressed in blue cordoroys, a white short sleeve Polo shirt, and leather loafers, he seemed ready for a special event, except for his face. Red patches marked his throat and cheeks, and his pale blue eyes were sunken within the two darkened circles beneath them.

"Hey, Brian, how are you?" Sandy walked toward the bed, smoothing the blanket's wrinkles.

"Okay. I'm not doing this today."

"I know how you feel, honey, but you know it has to be done." She was lining up cotton balls now. "I've got someone I want you to meet." Sandy turned to introduce me, and I chose to take the lead.

"Brian, I need your help. I'm Maria. I've not attended a draw with you before so I need you to walk me through it." I hoped my direct tone and gaze would diffuse some of his anxiety.

"What do you mean?" He was skeptical, but his eyes had moved off the tray toward my face.

"I've heard this is hard for you, and I know I'm going to work with other kids who have a hard time, and I wondered if you could be the expert for me."

"Huh?" I had his attention now. Sandy had stopped fidgeting.

"Well, I'll show you what I mean. Sandy, you can bring the tray over. Brian, sit here." I patted the bed and got out my pad and pen.

"Okay, Sandy, I want you to prepare Brian's arm just like you would normally. Brian, you have a job to do. You need to tell me exactly what you are feeling and thinking each step of the way." Sandy gently took Brian's arm and walked him over to the bed. He sat on its very edge and kept his hands clenched on his legs.

"What did you say?" Brian asked, his head down, away from me.

"Sandy, can you clean his arm?"

She got out the alcohol swab, took his left arm without help from Brian, and began to palpate the vein.

"Brian," I said, "What are you thinking right now?"

His eyes were fixed on the spot Sandy had cleaned. His vein popped up easily, and stood out against his pallid skin. "I'm thinking how Sandy's good. She doesn't pull too hard like the other nurses."

"Great. Now keep talking to me." I seated myself next to him on the bed. Neither his head nor his eyes shifted away from that vein on his arm.

"Everything I think?" he asked.

"Yeah, like a play-by-play in baseball."

He said nothing.

"What now?" I touched his right shoulder lightly. "What are you thinking now?"

"Now she's taking the wet thing out of the foil and cleaning my arm."

"What do you think about that?"

"It feels cold. I don't like it. My stomach is starting to hurt." I pointed at his stomach, hoping to direct his gaze there. He didn't notice.

"Tell me about the hurt."

"It's down low and it's sore."

"Sore. Can you describe sore?"

"Now she's wrapping a rubber thing around my arm. I hate it. It pulls my skin." His gaze had not moved. His free hand began to pound on his leg. I chose to stop asking about his thoughts and keep him actively recording the event.

"What's happening now?" I asked.

"She's getting the syringe."

"Okay."

"What?" he cried. Brian grabbed his left bicep with his right hand.

"Just keep giving me the play-by-play. This will be the fastest draw ever."

"But I hate needles." He rotated his head side to side as he tried to face me without losing sight of the needle. Sandy hesitated, then looked up at me.

"Tell me what you hate. Which part of the needle do you hate the most?" Behind his back I nodded to Sandy to keep moving.

"She's sticking it in my arm," Brian began to shriek. Sandy had the needle in, blood began to appear in the vial. I raised my voice to meet his tone.

"Brian, just focus on what's happening."

"I hate it when she pulls back. She's doing that thing, I hate it, I'm not doing this." Brian's back stiffened. His right fist moved toward the needle. To touch him might trigger a reaction, but I was worried about his fist. I stood up to face him, attempting to turn his attention away for just a second.

"Brian, tell me about the pull back."

"Awwww. I hate this. Shit. She's gonna do it. Shit. Fuck you all. Shit. She's gonna do it."

"Do what, Brian? Tell me. What's she gonna do?" I prepared myself to grab his arm should he reach for the syringe. Out of the corner of my eye I could see that Sandy had one vial full and was preparing to pull it out.

"She's gonna pull that thing out with my blood in it. I hate that. It sucks on my arm. I'm not . . . screw you."

Brian threw his body back, ripped his arm out of Sandy's hands, and flung the syringe out. It rocketed past Sandy's face and shattered against the sink. Sandy jumped back but held the vial safe in her hands.

"Enough?" I looked at the vial.

"Enough for me. I'm not doing this again with him." Sandy glowered at Brian and walked out. Brian jumped off the table and ran to the corner, kicking the weight scale with his left foot.

"Brian, talk to me." I stayed near the bed, unsure of his temper and fear.

"Screw you."

"Stay here," I demanded. "I'm going to call your parents in."

I found them in the lobby and returned with them to the examination room where Brian was. I introduced myself quickly, my voice shaky.

"I want you to see the evidence of our attempt to draw Brian." I pointed to the broken syringe and then to Brian, now rigid in the corner. "The best nurse on this team will no longer draw your son. No psychologist has helped.

I don't believe my technique worked much better. Your son must have his blood taken regularly. This is not working." His parents were staring at me. It occurred to me that they had not received the staff's anger directly before. I pressed further. "We cannot draw him again without sedatives. It is too upsetting for him and too dangerous for our staff. He is tremendously anxious, and that must be addressed. Can you agree now to sedatives?"

Brian's father shook his head vehemently.

"Then you may have to consider taking him to another hospital." My stomach tightened.

I did not know if these people knew that I had just said something outrageous. The authority to suggest another hospital was not mine, but I did know that it was unfair to ask the staff to tolerate such behavior.

Jordan and his wife, Sally, murmured to each other. Neither of them moved to comfort Brian.

"Your son is miserable. We can't ask him to manage this. What if that syringe had hit him or Sandy in the face?"

They kept silent. I tried one last gambit.

"You are his parents and even you won't be in the room with him. Doesn't that say something to you about how out of hand this has become?"

Sally searched Brian's face. "What do you think?"

Brian shrugged and I interrupted before he could respond.

"You are the adults. This is your call. Your son needs help. He cannot choose by himself about something so painful."

"She's right, Sally." Jordan's voice boomed. "Brian, move out of there. We'll agree to have him medicated, but I don't ever want you near him again. You are not to be his therapist."

"That's fine, I'll make sure he gets someone else." I turned to Brian then. His face had reddened into florid splotches. "I want you to know that it takes a lot of courage just to show up here after what you've been through these past months. I'm sorry you've had to suffer so much anxiety."

"I'm not coming back here," Brian said. Sally stepped toward her son. Jordan intervened, grabbing Brian by the arm. He pushed him to face the door.

"Right now we are going to talk to Mike." Jordan spun out the door, his hand clenched around the back of Brian's neck. Sally followed without a sound.

Twenty minutes later I was called to Mike's office. When I walked in I could see he was upset.

"What the hell did you do to Brian?" he asked. "His parents are furious. They're leaving the hospital." Mike threw a pile of rubber tourniquets onto his chair.

"I did the best I could, Mike. What I did was bring an untenable situation to a head by making them confront it. They didn't want that."

"They certainly didn't. Now I've got two angry people on my hands." Mike shut the door behind me and sat down. I could see him chewing the inside of his cheek.

"What about Brian? This has been horrible for him."

"Maria, a needle stick is a minor suffering to keep him well."

"I don't question that. What I question is how this has been handled . . ."

He interrupted and waved me out. "Take that up with Donna. I don't have time for psychological strategizing. Don't take matters into your own hands again without clearing it with me first."

I went to my office, dumped my folder on my desk, and left for a walk, angry at myself for letting the draw escalate and frightened that I had compromised Brian's care.

The Morrises returned one more time after another consultation with Mike. Brian was given Ativan in pill form and the blood draw passed smoothly. At the end of the visit, Jordan announced that he would be taking Brian to their local hospital from now on, yet wanted Mike to be in charge of any changes to the treatment plan. Mike agreed to accept responsibility for overseeing subsequent blood test results as long as Jordan had the results faxed the day they were taken. I received an official reprimand in a letter from Mike, yet the nurses thanked me for forcing a resolution.

On Friday of that week, I reviewed Brian's session with Donna while sitting in the intern room. As we discussed what might have been done differently, I found myself looking at the toys and textbooks and stuffed animals.

"Nothing in this room would have worked with Brian," I said.

"That's right. He needed to have his anxiety managed. You couldn't have done that through play therapy."

"But what I did was not great, either. He didn't leave feeling more in control. I suspect I harmed him more than I helped him."

"It doesn't always go smoothly, Maria. You're new to this. I could have helped you prepare better for this case." This was true and might have been useful, had I had the foresight and humility to ask for help.

"These kids shouldn't have to suffer because I'm inexperienced."

Donna inclined her head to the side. "We've all had that feeling. What made you choose to go for the draw immediately?"

"Isn't it better to take action than not?"

"Not always. What makes you think that?"

I had no answer.

Four months after Brian's last visit to the hospital, I would watch a documentary about young children with kidney disease. The interviewer, a woman in her fifties, appeared to be captivated by a ten-year-old girl, Jennie, who had decided she no longer wanted dialysis. The documentary followed Jennie in her last weeks of life, as well as the lives of four other children in various stages of disease. Organ transplant was not an option for Jenny. Though her parents appeared devastated, Jenny beamed. In one shot, they captured her swinging at her elementary school playground. The interviewer asked, "What was the best part of the past year?"

Jennie took a moment to swing-kick herself up one

time, then let herself slow down, breathing hard. "Not having to take medicine anymore."

"And what was the hardest part?"

"Having to go to the hospital a lot."

I turned the TV off. I knew then how much damage I had done to Brian. He had had a choice that I had not seen: the option to walk away from monthly draws and simply live. What harm would it have done to wait three months or even six months for the next blood draw? He had been healthy, in remission. A few months away from chemo and the hospital might have changed everything for him. I hadn't seen it. I could not have imagined saying no to standard medical practice or altering the pace of treatment to spare a child's psyche.

Medical practice, truth be told, is art as well as science. I had faith back then that what medicine had to offer in terms of drugs and its formal, regimented protocols, was not only the best thing but the right thing for cancer patients. Yet only four years later, in 1997, my husband, Jonathan, would choose chemotherapy *and* alternative methodologies (energy work, herbal supplements, meditation, and acupuncture) to cure his Hodgkin's lymphoma and I would support his choice. In that intervening four years, counseling adults facing not only cancer, but heart and kidney disease, diabetes, and chronic asthma, I came to understand what the mind-body folks had figured out: that medicine is but one approach to illness. Psychological wellness and physical health often both improve when the client is encouraged to explore multiple options. There is no one right way to heal.

Today, even medical professionals agree. In the last ten years I have overheard countless physicians imagine the day they could give up the "barbaric regimes" of chemotherapy and radiation in exchange for much less destructive therapies. Survival rates for pediatric cancers have never been better—up to 65 percent for most cancers—but children subjected to current therapies may pay a high price later on in life: heart disease, secondary cancers, learning disabilities, infertility are all possible consequences. Physicians understand this toll and look to gene therapy and stem cell research as paths toward future nontoxic, noninvasive treatments. "Oh for a stronger magic," wrote doctor-poet Richard Berlin in *How JFK Killed My Father* in response to a patient's incurable cancer, "that I could wave my arms, and reach deep inside my white coat pocket, the mass vanished, my hand a heaven of diamonds." Physicians, working every day within the limits of scientific knowledge, knew better than I that not all we have to offer works.

The larger field of medicine itself has changed since the early 1990s. Hospital administrations have broadened the scope of care. Major treatment centers and some local hospitals today offer patients opportunities for participation in stress reduction classes, therapeutic touch, support groups, nutritional counseling, and acupuncture. As a public speaker I am often invited to talk to physicians and nurses about the value of paying attention to what one's heart needs in order to navigate through illness.

But as an intern, new to the field and scared to make a mistake, I believed firmly in the protocols given by the doctors and believed physicians knew what was most effective for patients. Now I would know to suggest to Brian's doctor that the boy's blood draws be scheduled to give him time to adjust—to help, in effect, heal his spirit.

5
A Peaceful Dying

Her first day home from the hospital, Lily and I spoke briefly. She complained that the pain in her head was bad, and she wanted it to go away. Her mom and I consulted with the hospice nurse, and I helped Celia articulate her daughter's request for no more pain. Celia wondered if it would be okay for Lily to sleep downstairs in the kitchen. She explained that Lily had become foggy since coming home, but had asked clearly not to be left alone. I told her it would be perfect to have Lily surrounded by the comings and goings of her family, as long as it didn't seem to exacerbate her pain. They moved her into a hospital bed in the kitchen, where she could be amid the chaos of her siblings and the family dogs and where she was never without company. Over the next three weeks they all lived in that kitchen. The younger children took turns playing and resting on mats on the floor near her as if they were her honor guard, and Barry moved his recliner into the entrance of the kitchen pantry where he half slept each night.

How one does this, sits vigil by a dying child without

breaking apart, was a mystery to me. For the twenty or so days that Lily lingered I imagined what it might be like for Celia and Barry and could only allow myself to stay there for moments at a time. "We do what we can," Celia had once told me, "to keep living while getting ready for her death." More than once I wished that I could be in their home, near Lily, learning from all of them how to do just that, to be in life while someone you love dies peacefully at the same time.

I did not speak to Lily again; morphine kept her pain free, but silent. One morning two days short of Celia's birthday, the children took turns reading to Lily from her favorite book, Madeleine L'Engle's *A Wrinkle in Time*. In it, a young girl, Meg, conquers evil by remembering what it is to love herself and others in her own unique way. Lily's eldest sibling, Carrie, called me at eight that evening. They had finished the book, and Lily had seemed to smile.

"Do you think that she was feeling better?" Carrie asked me.

"Yes," I answered. "Her body is not better, Carrie, but I'm certain you've nourished her spirit."

Just before sunrise, the next morning, Lily died, surrounded by her father, her sister Carrie, and two snoring spaniels.

For the next four nights I lit a candle for Lily as I lay in bed, and watched it quietly for a few moments before blowing it out, a holdover from my Catholic childhood. I spoke to the air above the flame, telling Lily it was all okay. Longing for her to be cared for, I invited her ancestors to find her and escort her. On the fourth night, I realized then that I had no place to put her. Where would such a child go? Images from parochial school—heaven, hell, the judgment gate, purgatory, limbo, or angels swooping to gather innocents who died before they could sin—no longer made sense to me.

Celia, I knew, dreamed of a house for her daughter, with one great room and many bedrooms where Lily would wait, reading her books and writing of heaven's creatures until Celia and Barry and each sister, brother, and pet joined her. But I no longer knew where to put my dead.

On break, five days after her death, I walked to the Riverway (a walkway along Brookline's Muddy River, adjacent to the hospital) to think of Lily. I sat against a willow embedded tenuously at the river's edge. Lily taught me that dying, even for a child, can be peaceful, and that death itself need not be a torment. I wanted to hold on to this knowledge and hold on to her by finding a place where I could see her in my mind. The river eddied around the tree's roots and I felt attuned to what it must have been like in her kitchen, surrounded by love. After a time an image came. In the water's scattered light I saw this: a round white room, opened to Earth and to blue, and a girl surrounded by light and dust motes bending down to observe all that was happening below.

*   *   *

It is 2002. An elderly woman, my therapist, is dying eight weeks after the diagnosis of lung cancer, which has metastasized to her brain. She calls and we speak for the last time. In a poignant reversal of roles she describes to me what she is experiencing: the sense of peace she feels in some moments and the fear in others about what will come in dying. She knows what I have learned and asks me for guidance. I invite her to surround herself with those she loves and those she feels safest with. I suggest she place herself in the warmest, most welcoming spot in the house and I tell her about Lily—about the kitchen and the dogs and the recliner. I learn later that she died quietly, her daughters nearby, her husband asleep next to her, the poems she loved scattered about, and lilacs scenting the room. Nine years after Lily's death, her life brought a gift to another.

6
Kindness Always Helps

Adjacent to the cancer center sits Children's Hospital. To its left lies Beth Israel Hospital and a nurses' teaching college. Brigham and Women's Hospital faces the cancer center's front, five or so blocks away, and to its rear is New England Deaconess Hospital. Forming a ten-block hub, each building is now connected to the others via underground tunnels and elevated glass walkways. But in 1993, we visited staff at the nearby hospitals via the area's often windy streets and sidewalks. Patients, physicians, and staff were allowed to park in underground lots, while we interns struggled to find parking and face the wind. Frequently I would meet my colleagues at Dana-Farber's front door, all of us with heads bowed, files pressed against our chests, looking forward to entering into the relative warmth and calm of the lobby.

One especially nasty morning I had trouble getting through a door. I had walked over to neighboring Children's Hospital, which housed the bone marrow transplant unit and where our pediatric clients were cared for pre- and posttransplant. Carrying files, a briefcase loaded with a draft of my dissertation, my pager, wallet, and some children's books, I caught my heel and was thrown toward the hospital's glass doors. Spilling most of what I carried, I found myself assisted in the cleanup by Daniel Berlin. Dr. Berlin, head of the Bone Marrow Transplant (BMT) unit, was an internationally recognized expert. Children were flown from India, Africa, and England the year I worked at the hospital, in order to be under Daniel's care. That morning he was almost unrecognizable given that he was wearing a Santa Claus outfit.

"Are you in the school play today?" I asked, joking once we were inside.

"I do this every year. The kids love it."

"You're kidding. Aren't you Jewish?" I peeked inside the cloth bag he had slung over his shoulder as we waited at the elevator. Brown, red, white, pink, and blue plush creatures nestled together, amid bags of candy.

"Doesn't matter. We go for whatever helps here. Go ahead; quiz me."

"What do you mean?" I had taken the bag from him and opened its mouth fully to get a count of his generosity. Twenty-three stuffed animals.

"Ask me Santa trivia." He tapped his head, as if to jostle a memory box.

"Okay, name the reindeer."

He rattled them off, in order, and even sang "Rudolph the Red-Nosed Reindeer." The elevator doors opened. I entered to go up to the bone marrow unit while he waited for his ride down to pediatric ICU.

On the way up the elevator picked up His Highness,

Larry Mott. His Highness, my nickname for the hospital's youngest pediatric surgeon, and I did not get along. I had caught him one day discussing my six-year-old client's leg amputation as if it were going to be a great event for him. "Yeah, the little ones love me. They think I'm God if I save even a little bit of leg for them." Insulted by his callousness I had asked him, in front of his resident, what he was going to do for an encore that day. He snorted and turned away without answering. We spoke only when necessary after that.

Callousness in a physician as a defense against the onslaught of suffering was not new to me then or now. Lecturing at Williams College in January 2005 to premed students, I learned that one of their greatest concerns was the fear that they will become hardened or exhausted in the face of constant suffering. They know this is a possibility because of what they have already seen in the field and what they have read. The literature is filled with such examples: pediatrician Rachel Naomi Remen in *Kitchen Table Wisdom,* being told by her senior resident that it had been inappropriate for her to cry with parents who had just lost their only child; surgeon Bernie Siegel in *Love, Medicine & Miracles* debating whether to change his specialty after years of having learned professional withdrawal in order to hide his empathic suffering with his patients—a tactic which kept him disconnected from the very patients he wanted to help and from his heart; family practice physician David Hilfiker in *Healing the Wounds,* describing the hidden realities of physician addiction, suicide, and mental collapse in a profession that does not teach its practioners how to handle the vulnerabilities of being a human being watching others suffer. And Paul Farmer, general practice physician and advocate for the Haitian people, describes in Tracy Kidder's *Mountains Beyond Mountains* how hard it is to get other doctors to give of themselves fully in the presence of unremitting pain and poverty.

The Williams students had their own personal experiences with doctors who had disconnected from their hearts or found other ways out of dealing with the pain. I too had seen a friend choose to leave a high-profile hospital as head of the internal medicine department after his addiction to the drugs he prescribed was discovered; a colleague who left the pediatric speciality he loved to become an emergency room doctor after a teenage boy died while under his care; a heart surgeon who moved to a small-town hospital from a prestigious teaching hospital after he found himself drinking each night postsurgery to dull the pain. "The pressure," wrote Siegel, "never let[s]up."

Daniel Berlin's generosity had made me happy and feisty, so I greeted Dr. Mott cheerfully and told him about Santa Berlin.

Larry laughed. "That's nothing. Wait'll you see me as the Easter Bunny."

"I'd pay to see that," I volleyed.

"You might have to," he returned. "Where are you headed?"

"Bone marrow."

"Ah, where the rubber meets the road and the bone is laid bare."

I nodded. Crude as it was, he was right. Bone marrow transplant (BMT) was a last resort if disease had returned following treatment. Sometimes, when all other options had failed, transplant was the only remaining chance for a child's cancer to go into a more durable remission. Yet it required great risk: removing a child's marrow and replacing it with new marrow left the child with a suppressed immune system that sometimes failed beyond repair.

I got off the elevator on the BMT floor where most of my clients were. Though I wasn't scheduled to see anyone until midmorning I preferred writing notes in the BMT nurses break room.

The BMT wing was L-shaped. Patient rooms lined both sides of the corridor on either leg of the L. At the juncture sat the semicircular oak-paneled nurses station where two nurses could fit comfortably, answering phones, handling charts, sending innumerable pages. A single doorway behind their desk led to the physicians conference room. There, seated in stiff-backed chairs around a mahogany conference table, surrounded by portraits of former BMT chiefs, the teams met to hold new-patient briefings, discuss case strategies, and conduct postmortems

(case reviews held at the conclusion of a difficult or an unusual case). Doctors and nurses passed through the nurses
station ceaselessly. It was the floor's hub; even at midnight
it buzzed with activity. Yet the floor's heart beat in the
nurses break room.

Across the hall to the left of the nurses station, the
break room housed a round table that sat four, a small refrigerator, a microwave, a metal stand on wheels used
solely for storing soda, a coat rack, a rubber mat for boots,
and a bulletin board. Backpacks and purses spilled out of
the one cupboard that actually had a door. On other nursing floors the bulletin board carried hospital protocol
sheets, meeting reminders, security information, and rotation schedules. BMT was different. Its bulletin board
looked more like a refrigerator in a bustling home: photographs, party invitations, recipes, directions to houses, and
children's drawings streamed on and off the 3' × 5' board.
The formal debris of hospital life took up little room
there. The BMT break room was all about comfort.

After a mere two weeks of circling in and out of that
break room, I learned something about nurses: The good
ones buzz with competence and are dedicated to letting
patients know they are normal despite their abnormal diseases. The bad ones are punitive in subtle ways, implying
to the children that they are not working hard enough
to get better or suggesting that misbehavior would bring
about another illness. These nurses did not last long on
BMT, for the head nurse, Catherine, would not tolerate
anything short of loving-kindness toward "her" children.
I witnessed nurses under her guidance swap recipes with

patients' parents, help siblings draw get-well cards and share their sorrow, and on many occasions make a birthday party for the BMT kids. With Catherine and her staff, the difference between a child with hair, health, and freedom and a bald child, trapped and in pain, was kept as small as possible.

Catherine could be found most often behind the nurses station. Angular and tall, in her midfifties, she ran the floor like a benevolent abbess. Rules were clear and unimpeachable, but on Catherine's watch there was no need to be harsh about them. She reprimanded in private and praised in public. The children flourished under her smallest gesture. Nurses, once under her supervision, did not ask to be transferred.

I sat at the break room table near the open door. Josie, a BMT five-year veteran was scooping ice chips for a patient. We'd begun to chat about Santa Berlin when we heard an IV pole's scratch-walk outside the door. Diane, a thirteen-year-old new patient, shuffled by. Admitted that morning, she was scheduled to receive chemo for the next three days prior to her bone marrow transplant.

"Hey, Diane. You okay, honey?" Josie asked.

"Yeah, just bored. Do you know where my parents are?" the girl asked. I noticed her head drooped to one side and her shoulders slumped, as her left hand twirled her hair.

"No," answered Josie.

I chimed in. "Do you want me to find out? I imagine they are meeting with staff."

Catherine, overhearing this, stepped out from the station to come over and say, "They are downstairs with the social worker handling some paperwork. Do you want to sit with us for a moment?"

Diane's face brightened and Catherine helped her wheel the IV pole over the doorjamb.

She angled her free hand to keep her hospital gown, called a johnny, closed behind her and began to look around. "Wow. You guys have a lot of stuff in here." She had spotted the backpacks thrown about.

"Did you bring any of your personal things with you?" Catherine asked, flipping her stethoscope off her neck and sitting down, patting the seat next to her.

Diane slid into the seat sideways in small increments, adjusting the pole with each movement. "No. I mean we thought I couldn't really have anything with me because it all had to be sterile." She tucked the johnny under her buttocks and sat fully back against the chair to keep the gown closed. I remembered once almost losing a bathing suit bottom at a school pool party. A boy had tugged play-fully at its tie—I had not yet known enough to knot a string-tied suit when around boys in a group. The suit dropped to one side and I grabbed the loose fabric to pro-tect myself but my buttocks were exposed. For a brief mo-ment, before my friend ran over with a towel and while the boys taunted me, I was certain that my rear end had be-come monstrously huge. The simple fact of wearing a johnny made Diane, and her peers, feel vulnerable, not to mention what it must have been like to have their teenage bodies examined by teams of physicians, most of whom were strangers. I found myself wishing I had a blanket to offer her.

"It's true once you have your transplant we have to be careful," Catherine said, "but I don't see why you can't have something you like with you now."

"Like what?" Diane's left hand worked the skin on her right thumb, already swollen and red around the nail, clearly a habit she used to try to manage her anxiety.

Catherine continued. "Well, what do you miss from home already?"

Diane answered immediately. "I wish I had my beads with me. I make jewelry, necklaces and stuff."

Catherine and Josie exchanged a glance, and simultaneously voiced, "Amy."

"Who's Amy?" I asked. This was a name I had not heard before.

"I'll call her." Catherine jumped up and headed to the nurses station.

Josie responded. "Amy's a nurse who works the late-afternoon shift. She's always beading. She and Sandy bring their crocheting and bead bags almost every day."

Within seconds, Catherine was back with pencil and pad. "Write down what kind of beads and thread you like, and Amy will bring them in this afternoon."

"Really? Great." Diane started to write, describing to us seed beads and crystals, the benefits of silk versus leather versus wire thread. As she wrote, her left hand lay still; I noticed that each nail was bitten and raw.

Paul Movson poked his head in the door, nodding to Catherine. Catherine stood, placing her hand on Diane's. "Diane, you let me know what else you need."

"But what about the cost? I can't pay you for the beads."

Diane's eyes dropped to her hands. She bent her fingers into her palms. "We don't have extra money."

Catherine walked to the upper right cupboard and re- moved a blue plastic box with a latched lid. In the box lay odd dollar bills, quarters, a few fives and tens. "Whenever any of us has extra change at the end of our shifts, we stick what we can in the box. My roommate and I used to do this in college, and I kept the tradition here."

Josie interrupted. "We call it the fun box, and we spend it on things that make us happy."

"But it's for you and the nurses, right?"

"It's for all of us, honey," Catherine replied. "We all need things that make us happy." She gave the box to Josie. "She'll give you what you need when Amy comes."

Diane's eyes were wet. She stood up quickly and sur- prised us all by giving Catherine a quick hug. "Thanks."

"You're welcome. Come show me what Amy brings you."

"Okay, I will."

Catherine gave Diane a light touch on the shoulder, and Josie assisted her back to her room.

In five minutes, Diane's loneliness and fear had been abated. I made a note on the inside flap of my datebook, under the staff beeper numbers where I would see it daily, "Kindness always helps."

"Well, that's obvious," I whispered to myself, but left the phrase intact. Even the obvious can be potent on the right day.

7
The Antidote to Fear

Five days later I was back on the floor. Diane had had her transplant and was suffering badly. Her temperature was high and sores covered the interior of her mouth. She seemed barely cognizant and asked to be left alone whenever a nurse entered. Though she was not my client I worried about her, recalling the raw edges of her fingernails, her clear fear, and her gratitude for kindness. I went to check in with Catherine.

"How is she doing?" I asked.

"She looks pretty bad right now, but we've seen worse, Maria. It's too soon to tell." Catherine stopped copying the week's schedule to talk with me.

"Did she ever get the beads from Amy?" I asked.

"She and Amy made a necklace together that day. It's hanging in her room if you go in."

"I'd like to help her. What can I do?"

"She already has a psychologist, Maria. Sandra is working with her."

"I meant I'd like to give her something."

Catherine squinted her eyes. "Like what?"

"I have vials of beads myself," I began.

"Are you thinking of doing something with them for her?"

"I don't know what I'm thinking except that I wish I could help." My intention felt naïve, and I began to feel embarrassed.

"We don't encourage psychology staff to give the children gifts."

I nodded.

"However, we don't discourage it either, if you are so moved. Just consider what is appropriate and check with Sandra. You don't want to do anything to compromise her treatment."

"Alright, thanks."

I was unable to speak with Sandra for two days. She had been on staff for five years and was well respected for her cautious nature. She was careful, not prone to diagnose pathology until many sessions had been conducted. We met in the cafeteria for lunch where she told me Diane was fairly sick and her health could go either way. I told her about my initial meeting with Diane and my longing to help her in some way.

"If she were your client, what good do you think giving her more beads would do for her?" Sandra's question was an important one, and I didn't have an immediate answer.

"I'm not sure."

"It's easy at a hospital to want to give our clients the world because we say to ourselves, 'Oh, but she's facing death. She deserves every gift we can give her,' and that is true, but the gifts these children need more than any other is the gift of consideration about what will strengthen them in their experience of illness." Sandra rose slowly, pressing against the table with both palms. "Rarely do the tangibles help as much as our presence."

I repeated the phrase to myself, thinking I should write it down. Opening my datebook, I admitted to Sandra that I wanted to make a note of what she'd said.

Laughing, she pointed to the blank space in my book, "Then write this down, too. 'The antidote to fear or loneliness is not courage. It's connection.'" She watched me record the phrase and signaled me to follow her. As we walked she kept her hand on my shoulder. We parted at the reception desk. "I used to do the same thing, Maria. That's why I laughed."

"Writing it down helps me feel like I won't forget it."

Sandra tweaked my sleeve. "Writing it down means you're already taking it in, and that's a good thing."

I kept the vials of beads to myself. Instead I tracked Diane's progress daily. She suffered greatly, but one day, in her third week on BMT, her condition began to improve. It was her first day without fever and the nurses threw her a miniparty. I was on the floor, as was Sandra, and we were invited to come in. Six of us scrubbed and entered her room to offer her applause and cheerful eyes over our masks. We encircled the bed and raised our hands in a victory grasp. Josie held up a placard on which the nurses had drawn a purple smiling face and peach thumbs-up sign. Surrounding the face were signatures in primary colors; every nurse on the floor that day had come in to sign it. Diane glowed when they showed it to her. It struck me that they, who had been in the trenches with sick children for years, knew far more than I about appropriate giving. Connection and kindness—such simple wisdom.

Diane left two weeks later in successful remission. In a few months Catherine received an envelope with three beaded bracelets for her, Josie, and Amy. A note from Diane was included. Catherine hung the note in the break room with her own "good job, staff" added. Diane's note read,

> I don't ever want to go through another transplant. I look terrible and don't have much energy to get up, but my mother makes me go to school and I guess that is okay. My friends are nice to me. They carry my books. I have the necklace I made in my backpack. I bring it with me every day. I don't wear it because my skin feels pretty touchy still. But I like having it with me. I made these for you because you took care of me and gave me beads from your own money. You are nice people and good nurses. Thank you.
>
> Love,
> Diane.

8
Playing God

Ten ten a.m. was break time for the union workers, and every day the same eight or so staff would gather outside under the high steel Dana-Farber sign to smoke. Joseph, one of the cafeteria workers, often brought his boom box, which would fill the corridor between buildings with music. The security guards, serious men in their fifties and sixties, hated this and allowed him to play it for fifteen minutes only. Joining Joseph faithfully were a few maintenance workers, some nurses aides, and young women from accounting. Each day at ten fifteen and two forty-five, they appeared to smoke their Virginia Slims, Camels, Marlboros, and Pall Malls. Passersby would approach the entrance, see the group inhaling and exhaling under the hospital's sign, and walk away shaking their heads.

The irony of cigarette smoking at the hospital's entrance disturbed me. Friday afternoons were supervision time with our team, and I brought it up with Donna and my peers on a late-November afternoon, the week before Thanksgiving. By now our caseloads were full. Jason and I had had a child die the previous month, and Paula's youngest client, an infant with brain cancer, had been taken off life support that morning. Seated around the intern office, we all looked a bit yellow under the room's fluorescent lighting. I commented on our color and suggested *we* should start taking breaks outside if only to get fresh, smoke-filled air. Donna heard my sarcasm, yet took me seriously and asked me to go further with my thoughts.

"The cigarette smoking bothers me for the obvious reasons," I said, aware of my own voice deepening, a signal to myself that I wanted to sound authoritative but was on emotionally shaky ground. "But I know there's more to it."

Audrey sighed, "It's like it's unclean. It makes the hospital entrance dirty."

"And the problem with that is . . . ?" Jason asked, prompting me to go on.

"I just wish it were all clean, for the kids." My voice pitched low then high.

"Clean? As in perfect?" Donna asked.

An ache pressed at my throat. I shook my head; I couldn't speak.

Audrey sighed again, and we all turned to her. "I think I understand Maria. Can I try?"

"Go right ahead, girl," Jason responded for me.

"Well, I'll say it straight out." Audrey turned to look at Donna. "Some days, it is as if there is so little we can do, really, to make a difference, that if we could at least give the kids a perfect-looking place, well, maybe that would help."

"Even though it wouldn't," I said, my voice squeaking. I wasn't certain what I was struggling with internally.

"Even though it sounds silly, a part of me wants to believe that if the hospital were pristine then it might make a difference to the children." Audrey stopped. "Am I wrong?"

"Misguided," Jason answered. "Not wrong."

Donna swept her arm across the room. "You guys, this work, our doctors, are they not enough?"

"That's it . . ." I sat up in my seat, inhaling heavily to keep my nose from leaking. "I'm worried all the time that what I do isn't enough."

"And if you cleared the entryway of anyone who smokes, that would make what you do enough?" Paula chimed in. We were still too new to each other to be anything but socially appropriate, but her impatience with us was obvious. For the last few minutes she had been reading her client files, flicking the edge of the folder between her fingers. This was her second year in pediatric med/psych—perhaps she had already resolved this for herself.

"Hey, this is key stuff." Jason put his hand out, palm flat toward Paula's face. "Here's what I think. We are already a quarter of the way through the year, and we barely know how to help. We can't attack the cancer directly with meds or surgery, and that's frustrating."

"And again, we don't help?" Paula threw her folder to the floor.

Jason continued without pause. "Come on. You know what I'm talking about. The residents aren't always certain how to use us because they don't all understand therapeutic treatment. We know it helps these children and their parents to talk. But my sessions keep getting interrupted—vomit, pages, infections, fevers, you name it. Sometimes my one-hour sessions last less than ten minutes."

"You got it," I said. Jason was openly stating everything I'd been thinking privately over the last twelve weeks.

Donna glanced at us all as if to make sure we were all listening. "It takes time to understand your place and your job as an intern. The job is rife with obstacles, the ones Jason mentioned and other, larger ones."

The room was quiet now; we were with her so far. I looked out the window and saw glass and concrete and imagined a field with hockey sticks scattered on the ground. "Sometimes it feels like a zero-zero game," I said. I knew what I was feeling now. "Whatever vulnerabilities and strengths these children come with, whatever wisdom or pathologies their families demonstrate, cancer trumps them all. Part of the problem for me is that I can't help directly—I can't offer surgery or the latest cure, but also, no matter what I do, cancer derails the process, with fever, mouth sores, platelet drops, infections. It isn't even close to being straightforward therapy with these kids. The disease overrides it all. I can't ever get past a zero-zero game."

"Isn't cure enough of a win?" Paula challenged.

"But we don't cure; we aren't even really in the game sometimes." I rubbed my fist back and forth over my thigh, hoping it would stay the tears I could feel coming.

Donna extended her hand across her desk toward me. "Meaning what?"

"Meaning, that's the win," Audrey blurted before I could answer, "a meaningful life."

Donna smiled at her to go on.

"If you approach cancer in terms of beating it, the score is always going to remain zero-zero at best. You aren't ever going to feel confident that you will win because cancer may return, or it may take the next child. You heal one child, another one is coming through the door. It's endless."

I crossed my arms as if to defend against the truth she spoke.

Audrey walked over to the window; streetlights were coming on against the blue-black sky. "Einstein said the most important question to ask yourself is 'Is the universe a friendly place?'" She touched the air where an imaginary planet hovered. "Viktor Frankl suggested that in the face of suffering, can we change the question from 'Why me?' to 'Who am I in the face of this suffering?' or 'What meaning can I derive from this suffering?'"

Jason sat down next to me, pulling his sleeves down over his hands. "These are children, Audrey. We can't discuss larger-than-life questions with them. They are worried about whether they get to keep their limbs or if they are going to spend the next day in isolation."

Donna shook her head, directing her gaze at Jason. "The principles still apply. What is it that gives a child a sense of safety in her universe? What is it that helps a child remember who she or he is in the presence of illness? Audrey is offering you a way to consider psychological health irrespective of illness."

"Okay," I said. "I can do that, but . . ." It was hard to

admit how much I wanted to make it all better for the children. I knew what Donna was asking. Phrases from my first year at graduate school came to mind: unconditional positive regard, constancy, a secure holding environment, mirroring—theoretical terms intended to create a world in which a child could begin to feel certain that care would be constant, that safety was ensured, and that those around her saw her and understood, for the most part, what she was thinking and feeling.

Donna glanced at each of us. "Go back and review your texts tonight. Remind yourself what creates safety and a basic sense of self in a small child. Focus yourself there and see how that helps you in your work."

"Win-win, lose-lose, that's for the doctors to worry about. Is that what you're saying?" Jason asked.

"As difficult as that is, yes. In a medical setting, let the doctors worry about the final outcome. You worry about the child's sense of self."

"It's hard to not be able to affect it all," I said, tears flowing, "to watch them get sicker and sicker and not know how to help their bodies."

Paula stood up, came over, and squatted down in front of me. "You aren't talking about just fixing a kid, are you?" She paused. I stopped breathing. The whole room seemed to be listening. "That wouldn't be enough. You want to beat the disease itself." The room began to spin. I couldn't tell if I was rocking my body back and forth or if I was dizzy.

Paula pushed herself up, turning her back to me. She said, "Every professional faces this, Maria. Every doctor, psychiatrist, psychologist, nurse, and social worker learns this one truth at some point." She held her pager up to the desk light, checking its screen for something.

"That we can't do it all?" Jason asked, moving behind me.

Paula turned to him. "That none of us is God."

9
Singing Through

Right before Christmas I was assigned two teenage clients. Twelve-year-old Conor Ward, eldest of four brothers, arrived at the Bone Marrow Transplant unit first. His blood levels, scans, and chest films all looked just fine upon arrival. His new marrow was a near-perfect match. He had attentive parents, loving friends, and an optimistic nature. The staff expected him to cruise through transplant, and we planned for a three- to four-week stay at most.

Conor and I talked baseball, Boston Red Sox baseball. I learned about the short outfield wall, home-run slugger Mo Vaughn, the spirit of Carl Yastrzemski, and the amazing arm of Roger Clemens. Our conversations happened while Conor played baseball on his hand-held computer or over the din of great old sports moments being replayed on videos. His father, Walt, often brought him tapes of outrageous or incredible moments in the history of the sport. Walt had quit his job to care for Conor full time while he was sick and had dedicated himself to bringing his son anything having to do with baseball that would keep him laughing and inspired. Small, dark-haired Conor planned on being a shortstop. Walt encouraged him, telling him that heart and talent made a big difference even for a little guy.

On the wing opposite Conor was my other teenager, Marianna Ciepella. Seventeen years old, Marianna treated the hospital as a home for wayward girls. Having been in and out of the place for over two years, she no longer cared who she offended. Light-eyed and green-haired, she weighed nearly two hundred pounds. Torn T-shirts, fishnet stockings, fake leather miniskirts, and work boots were her signature outfit. She had pierced and tattooed her body everywhere—before sarcoma showed itself—and would tease the new residents, asking them to bet her fifty dollars whether or not she had a pierced clitoris.

If Marianna did not feel like being taken care of by me or a nurse on a given day she would greet us with a "Get the fuck out of here," when we walked into the room. Once, when I was feeling brave enough to try to talk her into a therapeutic discussion, she threw a bedpan at me—not the light plastic kind that most hospitals use but a heavy white metal one with rolled but nonetheless sharp edges. The pan hit me on the nose and scarred me for a few weeks. Marianna laughed at me each time she saw me after that. (I nicknamed her "the Buddha," because in her presence it was everything I could do to remain compassionate.)

Removed from parental care at age eight for neglect and suspicion of sexual abuse, Marianna lived with an aunt and uncle, Joanie and Paul Santarisa. She had attended school until the age of twelve and then began to steal and vandalize her schoolmates' property. At fifteen she was placed in a local residential care facility for teenage girls, which, according to Aunt Joanie, had made her even more angry and less caring about others. But Marianna and I learned something about each other that few people did, and because of that she generally tolerated me.

One afternoon when the floor was quiet I had stayed late to write notes. Most of the children were resting, and the nurses were in a meeting in their break room, with the exception of Christine, who sat behind the central station. I chose to sit in the conference room near the end of the hall, next to the stairwell. Few of the children were placed in this part of the floor. It was dark and smelled slightly of mold, like a wet basement. Marianna, in her contrary way, had asked for a room down here so she could be alone.

I sat writing notes about a ten-year-old girl, a child from another state, who had been moved to the BMT unit. She had no family accompanying her. They had flown back to the Midwest without notice after her last relapse. Paula and I had spent the morning helping the nurses try to find other relatives to care for her.

As I wrote, I noticed a high soprano voice, a voice of such delicacy that I thought at first an opera was playing on a radio somewhere. I listened closely and began to decipher the phrases being sung: "There has to be something more for me/There must be more than this provincial life/I want so much more than they've got planned." I got up to look and went to the nurses station thinking that Christine had turned on a radio. No music there. I went to the children's playroom, then Conor's room: nothing. I walked back to the conference room and remembered Marianna. I carefully approached her door and saw Disney's *Beauty and the Beast* playing on the TV suspended from the ceiling. The sound was off. Marianna was singing each word from memory in a voice that soared. On her face were tears, and in her hand was a worn paper rose that she must have hidden in her bedstand, for in months of treatment I had never seen it. She saw my reflection in the window of her door. She stopped abruptly, stuffed the rose under her pillow, and yelled, "Fuck you, if you ever tell anyone I sing, I'll get my brother to kill you."

I stepped in and begged her to continue. I told her the truth, that it had been a rough day. "Marianna, please, don't stop. Your voice is unbelievable."

She just stared, then signaled me out of the room with a head flick. But as I turned, she began to sing softly.

From that moment we became connected. I knew her gift, she knew I could be vulnerable. I left the room, slid down the wall next to her door, and sat. For almost an hour she sang.

10
The Need for Love

Cindy Striker, the ten-year-old whose parents had left her without notice, was not my client, nor any of my colleagues'. Her parents had chosen not to work with the psychology staff and had only a cursory relationship with the social worker assigned to them. We all knew about this girl, however, because the nurses asked for our guidance daily regarding her case. At first the parents had seemed interested in their daughter's care, but when Cindy's body failed to recover, they became difficult to reach. They missed appointments with the resident in charge, failed to sign permission slips, and once disappeared for two days without warning or a forwarding phone number. When it became clear that their daughter would not survive her lymphoma, they left, telling the staff that they had said good-bye and that it would be better for other family members not to bring their daughter home to die. What kind of love was this?

The year prior to my hospital internship I witnessed a similar abandonment by a parent. I worked at a community mental health center in the poorest section of Boston. Violence was prevalent there, as was robbery. Local schools had armed security guards at their doorways, and a metal detector had been installed at the high school's main entrance. My supervisor for the year, Evalise Navarro, had dedicated her life to working with the young women of this community. She warned me to leave my jewelry at home, carry only as much money as I needed each day, and leave the mental health center promptly at five. I lived and worked in jeans that year, bringing with me only my car keys, my driver's license, and two dollars in my right front pocket—just enough to take the bus home if my car was stolen. My task was to meet weekly with young mothers, ages thirteen to twenty-one, whose children had been removed to foster care due to the mother's use of drugs and/or alcohol. The mental health center had been given a grant to educate these girls about how to care for themselves, get off drugs, and manage eventually reuniting with their children.

My oldest client that year was a twenty-one-year-old named Denise May. Born to drug addicts, she had been forced into prostitution as a ten-year-old by her father to help pay for his cocaine habit. At fifteen she became pregnant; by the time she was nineteen her son, Tay, had been placed in foster care. He was returned to her care when she was twenty, and now, one year later, the Department of Social Services (DSS) case worker was planning to remove the child again. Denise had failed her last two drug tests. My job was to meet with her, every day if necessary, to support her in getting drug-free again.

I met with Denise for less than two weeks. Wearing torn sweatshirts, filthy jeans, and unlaced high-tops, she showed up for each appointment within ten minutes of our agreed-upon time drunk. She actually seemed beer soaked: her hands were sticky to the touch, her hair matted, her ankles filthy. Each day for the first week I talked about the DSS warnings, the loss of her son, and how we could help her get off drugs, and each day she'd smile, say little, and sometimes pass out. Twice that first week I had to ask a security guard to escort her out; I could not lift her myself. As the second week began I explained that DSS would remove the child on Thursday unless she showed immediate improvement. Tuesday and Wednesday were repeat performances. On Thursday, Denise failed to show, and that afternoon Tay was again taken into foster care.

The following Monday, Denise showed up for our appointment on time, mostly sober. "Mostly sober" meant she had had a beer or two that morning, but she could negotiate her body and her mind fairly well. Her eyes were clear and her body looked as if she had bathed that weekend. I said something to her in therapeutic language about noticing that she seemed to be in better shape than she'd been the previous two weeks, despite the loss of her son. Inside I was thinking, "Now you clean up your act?" with no small amount of judgment.

Denise flopped her legs over the chair, began to hand comb her hair, and speared my judgment within less than a minute. "You told me Tay would go if I was drunk. He'll have nothing with me. Now he's got a chance. Had to put on a major drunk to make sure of that."

Was it possible that Cindy's parents and Denise were similar, somehow convinced that their children were better off without them? Could this be a kind of love, or was it a giving up, a closing down of the heart in order not to feel their own suffering?

Most of the time a child's illness united his or her parents to work together on the child's behalf. By midyear I had come to know parents who slept in the child's room whenever possible, fathers who quit their jobs to care for their son or daughter, mothers who took on extra jobs to pay for the bills, older siblings who willingly chose to parent the younger children to leave Mom and Dad free to care for the cancer-struck child. Some parents and other relatives became experts at figuring out how to work the system, whether it be the social work system, the insurance system, or the system of relatives and neighbors to participate in the child's care. One teenager, whose mother was mentally ill, had an aunt who regularly brought her niece's schoolmates in to keep her niece connected to the larger world. And we often met grandparents who simply gave up whatever life they had been living and moved to be near the hospital to provide emotional support for their children and grandchildren. A few parents—like Celia, Lily's mom—became a surrogate parent to all the children, bringing stickers and books or sweets whenever possible to whoever was in the clinic on the days his or her child was there.

But sometimes—rarely—cancer and what it represented was larger than a parent's capacity to cope. A parent might begin using alcohol to medicate his or her pain, or become too paralyzed emotionally to even show up for appointments. Illness brought some couples to divorce, others to have affairs, and in some cases, like Cindy's, to abandon their sick child. When this happened, we all stepped in to help. Nurses offered extra attention, the social workers wove networks of support around the child, and we found ourselves playing out family dramas over Chutes and Ladders to help them articulate what parental loss meant to them. We'd visit our clients two or three times a day when they were in the hospital, check in with them at home, and question ourselves constantly about keeping therapeutic boundaries appropriate while doing whatever we could to demonstrate care to the child. We all wanted at some level to become parents to these children but we all knew that would not be the healthiest course of action. We wondered frequently, How do we heal a heart when a child is facing loss on top of loss?

I brought this question to therapists I knew who were studying therapeutic touch and energy healing with me under healer Rosalyn Bruyere. Sitting around a lunch table we discussed the dilemma of multiple concurrent shocks to an emotional system. Rosalyn, an internationally known healer with vast experience working with psychological and physical pain, overheard our conversation. We asked if she had a particular technique or energetic approach to healing trauma of this kind.

"Life is long," she replied. "Everyone suffers at some point and everyone suffers tragedy upon tragedy at some point. The question is not what to do with the client, the question is how do you keep yourself full when the cataclysm comes?" She took us all in as she spoke. "No healing happens when the healer is depleted. Fill yourselves. Then you'll be able to offer a great deal, even if it's only love that you offer."

I carried Rosalyn's words home with me. I knew her last statement was ironic, that she believed that offering love was no small gift to a suffering person. Healing, I began to understand after four months at the hospital, need not be bound by the tasks the children and I did together or the talks we had. When all else that I could offer as a psychologist seemed inadequate I could remember this: underneath the puppet play, game playing, pain management techniques, and therapeutic conversations, there could always be love.

11
Bare Bones

Two days after Marianna's serenade, I returned to the Bone Marrow Transplant unit to check in on Conor. His room was empty. He had been taken down to Pediatric ICU. When I asked the nurse what had gone wrong, she told me he couldn't keep his platelet count high enough to prevent bleeding. They had tried platelet transfusions but he was still bleeding internally. I was to go to the ICU.

To get to Pediatric ICU I had to go down four floors, down a long corridor, through a steel door marked EMERGENCY PERSONNEL ONLY, and into a large corner space divided into wall-less cubicles. The cubicles were separated by pale-green curtains hung by metal rings on hollow metal rods. The rings clanked against each other each time a curtain was pulled open or closed, and after two days a new person could judge the intensity of a moment by the clatter of the rings. Each cube had room for a bed, portable breathing equipment, a visitor chair, a permanent washstand, and a stool. The lights were bright, sometimes blindingly so. The nurses wore sweaters in pastel colors. No shade seemed deep enough to keep any of them warm; we were all cold there. Tones were hushed, harsh, and then whisper-soft, following the wave of a crisis. Even after the successful resolution of a crisis, there was never a celebratory cheer. We knew the next emergency was always just around the bend for some other child on the unit.

Here, movement was unstoppable. Hours passed without breaks for eating, bathroom, or air. The trauma teams were always coming and going; this specialist, that doctor, this technology, anything to save lives. But we never stepped in the same river twice. I learned not to make assumptions about what would heal or cure any of my clients. One girl whose brain tumor caused a fungal infection so pervasive it began to eat away at the tissue of her sinuses and nose, eventually walked out of the unit on her own while others who were expected to live sometimes failed before our eyes. Miracles did happen. You just never knew for whom or when.

Conor had been intubated for two days. Unable to breathe on his own, a breathing tube had been inserted down his throat, connected to a machine that sent him life-giving oxygen. He was in a coma, his body covered in layers of blankets. If we could do little else, at least we could keep the children warm. There were no sounds coming from his cubicle except the pulse of the equipment. His parents were standing off to the side, watching each breath. They were not touching, not speaking, but I noticed that they were leaning their heads toward each other. Danielle, Conor's mom, had lost so much weight that her pants hung loosely and her wedding ring was now on a chain around her neck laying against a simple gold cross. She signaled me to come over. She had a plan. I was to sit next to Conor and sing his favorite songs to him. She pointed toward a collection of tapes she had stacked on the washstand; country music, pop hits, nursery rhymes that must have been from his early years. "He likes to be sung to, so we've decided to sing to him until we can get him back to the floor," Danielle said. "You can do that for us while we are busy with the doctors, right?"

"Absolutely," I responded. I was relieved that they believed, like me, that children in comas might be able to hear, or at least sense what is being said around them. "What can I do for *you* two?" I asked.

"Pray," Walt stated.

"Pray?" I stumbled.

"You don't pray?" Danielle twisted her sweater with her fingers.

"I'm not sure anymore."

"You're Christian, aren't you?" Danielle had taken a step back, into Walt's body. I had unsettled her.

"I'm angry at God. Some days that makes it difficult to pray." My answer shocked me. I wanted to take it right back but couldn't. Danielle's question had brought us into personal territory that was difficult terrain for me.

Danielle was looking away from me now. "Why?" she asked, her head buried in Walt's shoulder, her question made imperative by the tremor in her voice.

Why, indeed. Here was a question I was not prepared to answer. I did not want to lie to or mislead Danielle. Yet,

I knew that watching children die had reopened a wound within me. It was Christmastime. Our staff had already lost four children and the training year was not yet half over; I knew there would be more death to come. My own childhood losses had been brought back to me—memories triggered by hearing the same words used for my cousin, my aunt, my grandfather used now with the children: "not much time," "nothing more we can do."

I stood silent, as novice clinicians do, afraid to not say enough or to reveal too much.

Walt rescued us. "Well, if you don't mind, what we were hoping for is just a simple prayer for his health. We're asking everyone we can."

"I'm happy to do that," I answered, which was true. I took Danielle's hand and squeezed it.

I found a stool and placed it close to Conor's head. I took a nursery-rhyme tape, thinking it would be easier for me to sing simple phrases first. I cocked my head and told Conor that I was here and that I would be singing to him for a time. I saw for the first time what it meant to have one's breath taken over by a machine, how the eyelids thinned so that it seemed you could see the eyes through them. Conor's skin tone had faded, as if blood was no longer reaching his skin. His nose looked pinched, his cheeks stretched, and for a flash, it appeared as if his bones had been bared, the skin had become that translucent. It crossed my mind to touch his nose and to feel, as with a dog, his temperature. He did not look asleep. He looked too tired to wake.

I held the tape player, but could not begin right away.

I turned to his parents and found myself tearing. "I'm so sorry he's here. I'll pray now if that's okay with you." I closed my eyes and offered a silent prayer. "Please God, not this child," was what came to mind. I repeated it over and over. After a few moments, sounds from the next cubicle brought me to. I pressed PLAY and began to sing. "She'll be comin' round the mountain when she comes . . ."

I sang to Conor for four days, for twenty minutes at a time. After each session, I met with his parents to discuss his condition. Nothing had worked so far to sustain his platelets, but the ICU team still had a number of options to try, so Danielle and Walt remained hopeful. On the fifth day, I entered ICU and checked in at the nurses station. The nurse there did not recognize me nor I her. Either she was new or a replacement for someone. "Who are you here for?" she asked.

"Conor," I said. "I'm his official songmaster."

"No singing today, and go quietly. They are saying good-bye." She looked away immediately.

It took a moment for this to register. I approached Conor's cubicle and silently peeked in. The intubator was gone, as were the IV poles and the heart monitors. Conor was lying flat on his bed, arms and legs tucked in, sheets pulled up to his neck. His eyes were still closed, but he seemed to have a bit more color in his face. For a second I thought, "Maybe this is okay."

Danielle and Walt were standing next to Conor, whispering. Walt rubbed his son's head. Danielle held a rosary up to her throat. Wrapped around her forearm, it had turned her fingers purple and blue. I moved the curtain slightly to alert them without making a large disturbance. Walt turned to me, shook his head, and waved me away. This was not okay.

I walked out to the hall and stood. Curtains were being yanked shut in the cubicle next to Conor's. A surgeon was at the nurses desk, asking for the morning report on his patient. A new resident was carrying files to the staff area. The desk nurse was on the phone. No one was free to tell me what had happened with Conor.

My pager rang. It was Marianna. She had asked a nurse to find me. I called the floor. Josie was brief, insistent. "Marianna's gone beserk. She just threw the residents out of her room, and now they are threatening to put her on meds for her anger. She won't talk to anybody until you are in the room."

My head swung around the room to take in the ICU one more time. Down the hall a team was moving a child out in a wheelchair. In Conor's cubicle a body pressed against the curtain, bulging it outward as if his mother or father had collapsed over him. My pager buzzed again. I headed back through the steel door, down the corridor. Images came to me of Conor teaching me to work a glove; Jake pinned down, moaning "no no no no"; Marianna's steel bedpan rocketing toward me.

12
Grief

The day after Conor died I could not work. My arm had jerked across my chest, waking me at five fifty a.m. I felt feverish, but my temperature was 98.5. My left leg shook while I showered and dressed. I sat to meditate but could not clear my mind of Conor's face. I called Donna and told her I was concerned that I would not make it through the day with other kids. She suggested I give the morning over to Conor and do what I could to face my sorrow directly.

At ten o'clock, having been restless for three hours, I grabbed my coat and walked the four blocks to the church in my neighborhood. My apartment building was one of many in a six-block area catering to undergraduate and graduate students and the young, newly employed. Its side streets were lined with small cheap cars: Hyundais, VWs, used Hondas and Toyotas, and an occasional station wagon. Competition for the on-street permit parking spots was fierce; many nights we simply left our cars and took the buses or the subway into the city in order to not lose our spot. The church, a multistory steel and glass structure, had a huge parking lot surrounding its four cross-shaped wings. On Saturday nights, visitors to our neighborhood frequently parked in church spots, knowing that as long as the car was moved before morning mass at eight thirty, the priests and police would leave it alone.

The lot was empty this morning but the church door was open, so I entered, approaching the votive candles first, the red glass holders reflecting five flames already lit that day. When I was a girl, lighting candles had been a favorite ritual, but my hands stayed at my sides as I stared at the flames. I couldn't remember why Catholics were supposed to light candles. Was it to pray for the sick and help souls reach heaven, or to pray for yourself?

I grew up with deliberate Catholics. My grandmothers both carried rosaries with them whenever they left the house. You never knew when a prayer would help. We prayed for the sick, for expedient house sales, for better jobs, for souls in purgatory, and for the starving children in Ethiopia. My mother's mother, Nonni, had a Jesus in repose in a lit glass case next to her bed. He was both Redeemer and night-light, a relentless presence. Attending church on Sundays and holy days was mandatory. We'd dress without speaking each Sunday, my brothers and I, our stomachs rumbling and minds theoretically cleared to receive Holy Communion. Our family would sit in the middle pews. We, like most of the congregation, were marked by our muteness, our rigid postures, and by near-perfect attendance, as if the anxious fear we all hid could be expunged by following the rules. As a girl, I loved the story offered me there in my parents' church: God sending an only child to redeem the world, impeccable behavior and dedicated prayer enabling him to return to the corporeal world. I'd daydream: I'd swirl around our church's rosestone flawless columns, invoke the Messiah in soprano, and he would respond, revisit Earth to absorb my pure supplication and sweet soul. When I walked to Communion I stuck my tongue out straight so the priests had no trouble placing the holy wafer, certain that the priests cared and that it would help save my soul. I always wore clean underwear on Sundays: God could see through, that I knew. Then my cousin Tommy died, and my faith, which had become tenuous when I was a teenager anyway, shattered.

Tommy was my mother's nephew, a first cousin of great charm. Five years older than I, he was the cousin who noticed how I wore my hair, how deep my tan was, how my curves changed over the years. Adopted by my mother's sister, Amelia, when his own mother abandoned him as a baby, he became the blond giant of our Sicilian family. Over six feet tall, he always appeared tanned and gorgeous to all our eyes. Some of his appeal lay in the fact that he liked what my uncles called "the party life." A beer was never far from his hand, a girl often sat on his motorcycle, waiting, and he lived mostly during the early morning hours.

His eyes were ocean blue. At family gatherings they

would find me, light up, and invite me toward him. Even with a date on his arm, he did his best to make me smile. It was with Tommy that I learned to flirt and dance. At family weddings, his ties were always off and his shirt open. I could feel his chest hair against my face. He would hold me tighter than cousins should and move his hips against mine, slightly, whispering secrets in my ear. His skin smelled like light summer sweat.

Tommy's brain tumor was bad from the beginning, malignant and inoperable. He was twenty-seven.

Mom would call often that year, as I was away at college. It was only a few months before the doctors gave up. I saw him once during that time and I recall nothing about my visit. It was easier not to remember what cancer was doing to him. At the end, I traveled to say good-bye to him in the hospital in Albany where he would spend his last week. His hair was gone. His head was swollen, and he seemed small in bed. I had never seen him curled up before.

"How are those boys at college? They treating you right?" he began.

"Yeah."

"You look good, honey. It's good to see you."

"Good to see you, too, Tommy."

"Bullshit! I look like crap."

I smiled then, which made him happy, and the aunts probably interrupted to keep any flirtation down, and that was it. I was afraid to kiss him and so stared into his eyes to say good-bye. The blueness was intact, as was his love for me. He let me go sweetly, as he often did, smiling and touching my hand.

It was ninety-eight degrees the day of his funeral. I wore a white dotted swiss dress with blue dots. It had spaghetti straps, fit tight around the chest, and had a matching jacket, which I did not wear. My bare shoulders, the underwear you could see through the dress, its tightness, all were deliberately chosen to piss the priests off, to say "fuck you" to God, and to please Tommy. He would have approved, but it didn't help. Tommy was somewhere in the ether, the same place as my grandfather; no dress mattered there.

I sat in the rear pew and looked around. Tall, arched stained-glass windows of the apostles and the great moments in Jesus' life lined the two long walls of the nave. My leg trembled steadily. I stared as the morning light, breaking through the colored glass, playing across Mary's marble face. She hung four feet above the floor to the left of the altar, behind an oak podium. Her head was bowed, covered in stone cloth draped like a nun's habit. Her hands were hidden in her gown, which fell to the floor and cascaded in folds around her bare feet. It was not clear what she was looking at so I walked to the front and angled my head to see what she would see were she alive: a worn carpet patch and the bottom of the podium. Only feet, I thought. What the hell is the point of that?

I moved to the far edge of the front pew. A musky smell

came through the open window to my right. A small casement window, it sat above an image of one of Jesus' final moments of freedom, alone in the garden after the last supper. The pew did not fit my back. I shifted closer to the window where I could lean against the end piece. I took my boots off and rested my bare feet on the kneelers' cushion, my leg knocking against the wood in front of me. I picked up a Bible. Its edges were marked by fingernail crescents. The outdoor odor increased and an image came of what was to come that weekend: a priest spreading frankincense over Conor's coffin.

"Everything is close," Rilke wrote, "and everything closing in on me has turned to stone . . . this terrible darkness makes me feel small." This is how we feel in the face of loss, tiny against forces we cannot control. I walked to the church to find the comfort I had there as a child and found only the power of grief, a cavern of stone pressed close. "If it's you, though . . . break in," Rilke continues, now talking to the Divine, "that I may know the weight of your hand and you, the fullness of my cry." It is what we all wish in grief, to have someone else or some greater being break through our pain, so that we are not alone and our suffering is seen and known and somehow transformed.

Tears fell onto my skirt. Laying my head back on the pew, I torqued my head so the sun cast its weak winter light directly into my eyes. I stared at its center, counted to twenty, and got up, my vision murky. Stumbling to the rear, I closed my eyes and held the edge of each pew as a guide. My aunt had walked like this the day of Tommy's funeral, unsteady, near-blind with grief. At the rear of the church I bumped into the water vessel. I bent over the marble bowl for a moment, opened my eyes, sank both hands in, and wet my face. I let the water drip onto my neck and throat. What solace here? I sank both hands in again, stood up, and walked out, holy water trailing behind.

For two weeks I attempted to settle my grief but could not. I'd wake in the middle of the night and not rest again till sunlight emerged on the horizon, dreams cut short by the alarm's blare. My stomach cramped and I dreaded each day at work. I jumped when my pager rang, frightened it would call me to another funeral marked by stuffed animals, and dreaded another return to church.

The religion of my youth had lost meaning for me. What I wanted could not be found there. I wanted Conor and Lily back. I wanted my cousin to be alive and my grandfather to have walked me to my first day of school. These were wishes I knew to be unreasonable, yet still compelling. I wanted to know how to live with my grief so that it did not burden the children I continued to treat at the hospital. I wanted to know how to care and keep caring without drowning in fear of the next loss. And I wanted and needed a different kind of faith—one that offered salvation in the here and now. By age thirty-two I had learned one true thing about myself—if being present to suffering was to be the work of my life I would need a way to face loss straight on while staying connected to the thrum of life.

13
Release

I took my journal to our neighborhood café to write in those two weeks, but sat for hours without moving. I could not read, or think, just stare.

The café had five tables and mismatched hand-painted chairs. Crookedly hung photographs taken by locals covered the walls. The café was owned by a woman with many young children who were often running about, and the place was managed by pregnant, single, twenty-year-old Peggy. Both women seemed to care that their customers had lives beyond the need for caffeine boosts. The flowers on the tables were fresh, cookie samples easily available, and making exact change didn't matter. I'd sit in the back at a pine table etched with wormholes. Stained dark, it allowed me to see the whole place while being undisturbed.

But I came here for another reason, also. One day, when I first began to work at the hospital, I ordered a cup of Earl Grey tea and noticed a card. It sat on the cash register, taped to the upper left-hand corner. Ivy vines on a white border framed a face preserved in plastic. It was a baby's face. The card was a blessing card, the kind you receive upon attending a funeral. I leaned over to read the dates. Born in May of one year, dead June of the next. Each time I ordered I sneaked a look at the card. One morning I could no longer pretend not to notice. I asked Peggy about it. She told me it was an accident, a drowning, she thinks, the owner's child.

I whispered, "How? In a pool? A lake? How?"

"I don't know," she murmured. "We don't talk about it."

I found myself rooted, and forced myself not to ask the question that I knew she could not answer: "Why?" Why this child, why that day, why any of us on any day?

After two weeks of ruminating I became edgy, irritable. My mind broiled. I kept returning to the café, thinking the company of strangers would cushion my sorrow and the normal rhythms of people meeting and sharing food would soothe me.

I was in the café one afternoon around three. A mid-January thaw brought a light that was pale yellow, a new-year sun strong enough to illuminate but not to warm. The adults wore sweaters, the children suffered under winter coats, and the teens opted for T-shirts and Polarfleece vests. The women in front of me could not decide whether to order hot soup or cold sandwiches, and I understood: it's hard to know where to stand in times of transition. Yet part of me wanted to scream, "Buy them both, buy it all, there's no time to fool around." I kept my mouth shut by squeezing my tongue between my jaws. When this began to hurt I practiced yogic belly breathing, a mistake, since it freed my mouth. "It doesn't matter. Just pick something, for Chrissake," I blurted. The women tightened their shoulders and tilted away from each other, looking at me over their shoulders. But they ordered quickly and left, whispering.

I slunk to my corner table and pulled out my journal, hoping to bury my chagrin in words, but I had not brought a pen. Unbelievable. Too embarrassed to ask for help, I shoved my book into my backpack and lunged out of the chair, knocking over a cappuccino on the neighboring table. I threw my napkin onto the spill, mumbling, "Sorry, I just lost something. I mean I've lost children, children I know died."

The café door slammed behind me as I tramped the three blocks to my apartment. I threw myself on my bed. My hip landed on a book I had bought the week before, in hope of inspiration: Annie Dillard's *The Writing Life*. I read every word until I hit page seventy-eight. I read it over and over, repeating it out loud until I could hear my voice clearly, and finally, for the first time since Lily's death and Conor's coma, release came. "Spend it all," Dillard wrote. "Shoot it, play it, lose it, all, right away, every time. Do not hoard what seems good for a later place in the book, or for another book; give it, give it all, give it now . . . Anything you do not give freely and abundantly becomes lost to you. You open your safe and find ashes." She reminded her students of the note found in Michelangelo's studio a few days after his death, a note left for his apprentice Antonio. It said, "Draw, Antonio, draw, Antonio, draw and do not waste time."

If faith is an ascension, a climb into belief first given by parents and elders, then letting go is descension, a precipitous fall to a rocky ledge—or a leap off a solid framework constructed when we were young, that had only seemed stable. I dressed at six thirty the next morning, placing a note in my pocket, my grief quieted. The note read, "Draw Antonio, draw."

14
A Child's Faith

I made my way past the lobby's fish tank to the psychology intern room, my note pressed deeply into my pocket. It was early, eight fifteen, and I hoped to orient myself before the press of pages and meetings began. I was glad to see that Jason was already in the office. I had come to count on him, on his kindness and predictable ways. A six-foot former lacrosse player, he arrived at work each morning by running the three and a half miles from his apartment and showering in the nearby college dorms. His cheeks always glowed from the run, and he began each day with a large hot chocolate, two donuts, and a banana.

"Got a new case." Jason's hello was always direct.

"Already? It's not even eight thirty."

"Donna left it for you a few days ago. She didn't want us to bother you with it while you were gone." The donut left some cream filling on his upper lip.

"Gee, thanks."

"You okay, Maria? Want to talk?"

"Tell me a good one."

Jason was a favorite on the staff for two reasons. He

offered sweets from his pockets, and he hoarded stories of the absurd and ridiculous like some people collect rocks. It was a trait I loved; it reminded me that life was strange anywhere.

"Okay, I told you about the guy with the lawn chair and the balloons, right?"

I nodded. Some adventurous fool had attached nearly thirty helium balloons to his lawn chair and had actually gotten himself up into the air above LAX airport where the air traffic controllers had to change flight patterns in order to keep the man from being hit. He was fined on a number of charges and awarded the Darwin award for that year, a tribute given to folks who try something so insane that they sometimes help the species by eliminating themselves.

"Okay, here's a good one. A trooper is driving along looking for a man who's been missing for a day or so."

"Oh, I know this one, about the guy who strapped a jet booster engine to his car, right?"

"Exactly."

Donna had come in halfway through and asked, "What?"

"Some kid decides to rig his car with an engine built to launch jets off aircraft carriers. He jerry-rigs it to the rear chassis, drives down a deserted road, and somewhere about three miles from a mountain range, flips the switch."

"And?" Donna asked, eyebrows raised.

"Shaboom!" Jason shouted, and then cracked up while packing Matchbox dump trucks into a bag for his session with a boy over in surgery. "He must have gone airborne after hitting a bump because all they found on the road were some tire tracks about a mile long. Three miles away and, I don't know, maybe 150 feet up, they find a burned-out hole in the mountain and small pieces of steering wheel. Little bits of car were scattered all over the valley. The guy was totally disintegrated."

"Let's not share this one with our clients today." Donna knew that Jason was prone to sharing these stories with staff in the clinic, to bring a bit of humor to the day. Once a teenager had overheard his story about a twenty-two-year-old stealing helium tanks from the Macy's Thanksgiving day parade committee, hauling them to a back alley, and selling helium highs until three a.m. when the parade committee, who had been searching the area frantically for their tanks, found them. The teen thought the story was a primer for a good time. His parents thought otherwise and complained to the medical staff.

"Okay, Donna. No problem, even though you know Bill and Rich would love this." Jason tipped his baseball cap to Donna and winked at me. "I'll be good and save it for rounds."

Donna ignored his teasing and walked over to give me a hug. "I want to know how you are, but I have a post-mortem at nine, and we need to talk about Amelia, your new client."

"Are you free for lunch?"

"I'll make time—how about twenty minutes, at twelve thirty?"

Jason chuckled. "Could you spare the time?"

Donna smirked. "For you, I have ten."

Josie met me at the nurses station and gave me a quick summary of Amelia Conlon's case. Age six, barely in school, she was returning to the hospital for aggressive treatment. Diagnosed as a baby with non-Hodgkin's lymphoma, she had been given a course of chemo and had been in remission for over two years. The lymphoma had returned two months ago.

I went into the small conference room at the entrance to BMT where her parents, Suzanne and Samuel, were waiting for me. On Suzanne's lap lay a folder two and a half inches thick. As I introduced myself I raised an eyebrow at the folder.

"It's all the articles we've collected about transplant," Suzanne said, offering me the packet. "We visited four hospitals before deciding to come back here for the surgery."

"Would you like me to know about any of these in particular?" I asked.

"Why don't you tell us about yourself first? We want to make sure you are a good fit for our daughter." Suzanne was a thorough and serious advocate for her daughter. By the end of their stay at the hospital she would fondly become nicknamed the "folder lady." She rarely appeared at a consultation with staff without data, research, or anecdotes pertaining to her daughter's care.

I began a standard introduction about who I was and how a psychologist could help Amelia negotiate the strain transplant inherently carried. After a moment, Suzanne stopped me. She held her hand up to my face and said, "You seem like a nice person. You might even be a good psychologist, but my daughter is quite special." Samuel nodded.

"How?" I said, "Tell me what you mean."

"She talks to God, to spirits." Suzanne leaned close as if to gauge my body's reaction to this news.

"Oh my."

"Would you like to hear a story?" She looked straight into my eyes.

"Please." I lay my pager down; my datebook and folder I slid underneath the chair. Suzanne told me she had received the call about Amelia's relapse in her car. The cancer had returned aggressively, and there was no option but surgery. Amelia was riding behind her and could sense that her mom was in tears. She held her hands out toward her mother and asked, "What's wrong?" Suzanne told her. Amelia responded quickly, "Don't worry, Mom." Suzanne railed, "What do you mean, don't worry? This is worse than it was before, Amelia. The surgery itself might kill you. I might lose you."

Amelia sat back in her seat and repeated herself, "Mom, don't worry. The cancer is not important."

Suzanne told me she almost ran off the road at this point. She pulled the car over and turned to face her daughter.

"What are you saying, Amelia?"

"The cancer. It's not why I'm here, Mom."

Suzanne stared. "What are you talking about, Amelia?"

"It's not why I'm here. I'm here to teach you to love better."

"Amelia, what are you saying?" Suzanne interrupted.

Amelia kept going. "When you learn that, then I'll go home again. Then I'll go back to God."

I looked down to make sure the hair on my arms was not truly standing straight up, which is how it felt. Suzanne sat forward, her hands flat on her knees. Samuel had his eyes closed and had slumped low in his chair.

"Tell me more." I was hooked, compelled by this girl's clarity of faith.

"Well," Suzanne continued, "yesterday when we were packing to come here, Amelia told me to call my best friend, Kathleen, in Hawaii. She said she had a message for her from Luke."

"Who's Luke?" I asked.

"Luke was Kathleen's son, my godson. He died a few years ago in a car accident. Amelia never met Luke or Kathleen. Hawaii was always too far away for us to get to. Anyway, I called my friend and put Amelia on the phone. Amelia told her that Luke talks to her at night and told her last night to tell his mom that he's okay but not to give away the arrowheads. I was on the other line. I could hear Kathleen crying. 'Are you okay? Does this make sense to you?' I asked my friend. When she could finally speak, she told me that Luke loved arrowheads and had a huge collection of them. What do you think of that?"

"How could Amelia know about the arrowheads?" I asked.

"Exactly; she didn't, except of course that she talks to Luke's spirit."

Of course.

"Does Amelia talk to other people who have died?" I asked.

"All the time," Suzanne answered, "all the time."

That afternoon I met Amelia. She was drawing pictures of flowers when I arrived. She had unpacked two yellow nightgowns, a black vinyl travel case for a Barbie, red reindeer slippers, and a diary. I commented that she had brought little compared to most children. Amelia responded directly, "I don't need much. I won't be here long." At that she put her drawing pencils away, opened the suitcase, and began to undress and redress her six Barbies. Her fingers were long and skilled at the fine-motor challenges brought about by tiny snaps and buttons. She could undress a doll without looking at it. I noticed that her hair, black and wavy, had not fully grown back in a few places. "Would you like my help, or should I just watch?" I asked.

"Whatever you wish," she answered. I sat back and we chatted about Barbie's new desire to sing in church on Sundays. Amelia was dressing the Barbies for choir practice. I explained that I would come by to visit each day, and we could talk or play games and that I could help her talk about her feelings. Her reply surprised me. "I have my mom for that, but if it's important to you, we can talk about feelings."

*   *   *

I met Donna for lunch and briefly recounted the pain I had been in following Conor's death, and we discussed Amelia's unusual history. She encouraged me to spend time with Amelia's parents as well as Amelia, noticing that talking about them intrigued me.

Amelia, however, wanted little to do with me. In the sterile room, posttransplant, she was not interested in my help. It was only in the four days before she was to go home, when she was back on the floor, that she agreed to my visits. She knew what she wanted and needed each day (Barbie play mostly), and once our play was over she was finished with me. I secretly hoped that our play would let me into her inner world where God and spirits were present to her, but Amelia kept that world to herself. So we braided Barbie's hair, dressed Barbie for the ball, had Barbie babysit younger children, and read to Barbie her favorite stories—all of which contained either a princess or a maiden in distress.

Thursday morning, twenty-four hours before she was to go home, Amelia decided to tell me a story.

She had begun the job of folding Barbie's clothes neatly into piles. Friday seemed imminent to her, and she wanted to be ready. As we sorted and folded together, Amelia asked me a question.

"When we came here, I heard you asking my mom if they thought the surgery would make me better," she began.

"I wanted to know if your parents felt comfortable with the doctor's choice to do a transplant," I explained.

"Why did you ask that?"

"I asked because sometimes it's important for me to help moms and dads tell the doctors what they really want."

"You didn't need to, you know."

"What do you mean, Amelia?"

"You didn't need to because it didn't matter what the doctors did. I was going to be okay."

"How did you know that?" I asked.

"God gave me a shield when I got sick. It keeps the bad stuff away."

"What shield?" I was confused.

"This shield, the one right in front of me."

All I could see in front of Amelia was a Barbie travel case, two naked Barbies, and four neat piles of clothes (beachwear, ballgowns, play clothes, and work dresses).

"Amelia, I don't see a shield. Can you show me again?"

"Right here, it's right here. If you look at me, you can see it." She gestured impatiently with one hand, up and down in front of her chest.

"Amelia, I think that's a shield that some people can see and some people can't. I don't think I can right now. Can you tell me what it looks like to you?"

"It's sparkly like white beads. It goes up to my neck."

"How does it work?" I asked.

"I don't know. God gave it to the angel, and she didn't tell me. The angel just told me to keep it on and it would make the bad stuff go away."

"So you knew you would be okay."

"Yep."

"What angel brought you the shield?"

"The big one."

"The big one?"

"There are big ones and little ones."

"Oh. The big one brought the shield for you." At this point repetition was all I could manage.

"She's the pretty one. Can you help me with this bathing suit? It isn't easy to fold."

And that was that. The pretty, big angel brought the sparkly shield from God to keep her safe. Not a big deal to Amelia at all.

When I left the room her parents were waiting for me. I told them Amelia's story, and Samuel spoke to me for the first time in fifteen days.

"God is as real to her as I am to you."

I dropped my head.

He continued, "Do you know that her favorite thing to do on the weekend is go to hear different preachers? Revivalists come to our area in the summer, and Amelia loves to sit under the tents and watch people swoon. Later she likes to go up to meet the minister and shake his hand. Isn't she incredible?"

"Her connection to God is extraordinary."

Suzanne took my hand. "I'm always glad when Amelia shares herself with others. It feels like it's one of the ways we can make the world better."

I squeezed her hand without speaking and turned quickly, their certain belief a knifelike contrast to my grief.

* * *

Donna met me in the intern room a few minutes later and I repeated the story Amelia had shared and watched Donna's face brighten.

"I've met some remarkable children," she said, "but I've not heard anything like this before."

"It is incredible."

"I'm glad you told me. The good stories always help when the bad ones come." Donna continued. "It reminds me of my art class."

"How so?"

"On Saturday my watercolor class met, and we talked about how some artists have one great theme that is present in their work no matter what form they choose, and other artists have multiple ideas, multiple themes. Their creativity just seems to expand. We're just a group of middle-aged dreamers. None of us has ever painted before, and we were laughing with each other, agreeing that we'd all be happy just to have one good idea to work with."

"How does this relate to Amelia?"

"Well, perhaps Amelia's story is the one good idea you'll be given this year."

My eyes teared up, vulnerable to Donna's care for me.

"Perhaps Amelia's faith and her clarity can work within you, like an artist's theme, and you can follow it and shape it and see where it leads you during the darker moments."

I felt too moved to speak. Jason and his roommate John walked in to pick up Jason's coat. He saw my tears, turned to John, and said, "I told you they beat us up here."

We laughed and all walked out together, shutting the door for the day.

Amelia belonged to that category of children too busy in their own lives to be bothered by cancer—children with optimism and a sense of purpose, kids with plans. In the late 1980s Erma Bombeck gathered stories of children surviving cancer in *I Want to Grow Hair, I Want to Grow Up, I Want to Go to Boise.* She noted these survivors for their resiliency, humor, and unsinkable belief that it would all work out. One such child would list the following in answer to a question a therapist asks about wishes. " 'My three wishes are,' " the child writes, " 'to grow hair, to grow up, to go to Boise.' " Boise or back to riding a bike, it doesn't matter for certain kids: life, like with Jake and Amelia, is in great part about doing what you love, now, today. My own daughter, Raphaela, showed me this, too. I took her aside the day she was diagnosed with severe asthma, following her eighth bout with pneumonia in two years, and showed her the nebulizer she'd have to use throughout the fall and into the spring and the medications she'd have to take each time she got a cold: Singulair, Advair, Rhinocort, and prednisone. I knew the medicines would change her temperament, her appetite, her ability to sleep. She, at age five, felt that I was bothering her; she had other things to do. "Mom, okay, but when are we gonna go ice skating?"

Amelia left the hospital fourteen days after surgery, Barbies and faith intact. I saw her again for her checkup one month later. She was completely cancer-free. We chatted briefly about the Barbies. Her collection had grown since she'd returned home, compliments of loving relatives. I inquired about the shield, asking if it still helped keep bad stuff away. She looked at me conspiratorially and motioned for me to put my ear close to her mouth.

"I gave it to my mom. She needs it more than I do."

"That was generous of you." I whispered. "What do you use now to keep yourself safe?"

"I don't need it anymore. It's inside me now. God says it's inside me now and it will be there till I get really old."

Amelia returned to school that spring and remained clear throughout the next six months. I lost track of her then as she began to receive checkups in her home state. But during the six months, whenever I saw her, I would wonder at the difference between us. To her, God was an ally. Her belief had been unshaken by cancer while my relationship remained damaged, a wound that would not heal. Would her story work, as Donna suggested, to reinvigorate my belief or was it a story too sweet to hold up against my uncertainty?

15
The Bus

One Thursday morning in early spring while I was with a client, Debbie Corio, and her mother, I got a call from Josie.

"Marianna's roaming the halls here. Can you come over and settle her down?"

Marianna had been readmitted for transplant. After two years of short-lived remissions her guardians, Aunt Joanie and Uncle Paul, had agreed to try the bone marrow procedure. On the floor for two days, Marianna had already thrown food at the nurses' aide, punctured an IV with a three-inch serrated knife thereafter confiscated by security, and hidden Catherine's stethoscope under a mattress for three hours the day before. Presenting her case during rounds that morning, we agreed that she was acting up due to the upcoming transplant. I had been asked to meet with her guardians to discuss a psychiatric consult. Acting out following a transplant could cost her her life.

"I can't come right now," I told Josie. "I'm saying good-bye to Debbie and her mom. I'll be there as soon as I can."

"Any suggestions?"

"Have her go down to the tape room and choose a Disney video. She loves them, but don't tell her I said so."

"Any particular one?"

"Anything with a princess and a monster in it will do."

"Whatever you say, Miss Lama."

I smiled and hung up the phone. I had told Josie how being with Marianna felt like training for monkhood through some crazy Buddhist practice. Every time I thought I could treat her with loving-kindness, she broadsided me with her temper. Despite this, I liked her and found it easy to spend inordinate amounts of energy simply to help her to act appropriately.

Cancer seemed almost irrelevant to Marianna, like Amelia, but for a very different reason. She had a personality dynamic that was so deeply ingrained it surpassed most events. She acted as if transplant was unimportant and caregiving unnecessary. Donna assured me this was absolutely untrue. We would have to find a way for Marianna to experience her fear and anger in a nondestructive manner.

I turned to Debbie's mother, Jackie. "Whenever you are ready, we can wheel Debbie to the elevator."

Debbie and Jackie had arrived at BMT one week earlier with an awareness that this was Debbie's last chance and that success was improbable. Her acute myeloblastic leukemia, AML, had not gone into remission through three chemo trials over eighteen months at her local hospital in the South. She had been unable to find a good marrow match, and her hometown doctors had informed Jackie that Debbie had no options left. Jackie was not ready to say good-bye. Despite the doctor's opinions, her husband's acquiescence, and Debbie's hopelessness, Jackie began to call the major treatment centers in the country. Our hospital was one of two that agreed to try to help Debbie. On a gray spring day, twelve-year-old Debbie arrived with her mother at the Bone Marrow Transplant unit. On her chart cover was a confidential note written to me after her initial meeting with the resident. The note read "Patient depressed, unwilling to discuss medical or therapeutic treatment. Outlook hopeless."

Typically I chose to meet my clients before reading their charts. I wanted to see them with unbiased eyes and create a moment for them to reveal themselves without prejudgment. The resident's note concerned me, and I thought it might be better to know Debbie's history if she was uncommunicative. The medical notes were concise. She had never met the technical line for true remission. Bone marrow transplant was not recommended, as a good match could not be found. Experimental trials from Europe had been discussed but rejected. "No further treatment" had been suggested three weeks earlier by her oncologist in her home state. A social worker added the following notation: Lewis, Debbie's father, had withdrawn after the first round of chemotherapy and failed to show up at subsequent appointments. He had informed Jackie that Debbie was to be her responsibility. He would take care of their two younger children.

The day of our first meeting, I viewed Debbie through

the entryway window to her room. Washing at the scrub sink, before entering, I could see that the light-blue johnny hung loosely on Debbie's shoulders. She lay still, on her side, facing away from the door. The freckles on her neck and back appeared black against her colorless skin. The skin on her elbows was loose and wrinkled, as if she had lost a lot of weight. The skin on her legs looked raw, almost cracked, and her ankle was bruised on the bone. She wore no underwear. As I entered, I knocked, said "hello," and closed the door deliberately so that she would know someone had entered. She did not move, not even to cover her buttocks, an unusual lapse for a twelve-year-old.

I pulled a chair up close to the bed and introduced myself. Curled into her chest were six horses—four plastic ponies and two brown mares. One was velveteen; the fabric had been rubbed away around its neck. Two ponies had broken legs, and a third had no tail.

"Those ponies have traveled far!" I opened.

Debbie kept her eyes closed and remained still.

"Debbie, I'm here to spend some time with you if you'd like. Sometimes it helps to have someone to play with other than your mom."

She pulled her johnny shut then and rolled away from me. I saw that her other ankle was also bruised.

"Debbie, I imagine it must be sad for you to be here away from home. I'd like to help. We can talk, or play, or draw—whatever would feel right."

"I'd like you to go away," she whispered and hid the horses underneath the sheet.

"I heard you, Debbie. I'll leave now and spend some

time with your mom. I'll come back to check on you later." I had walked around the bed to say good-bye to her and knelt down to be at face level. Something stood between us, sorrow or terror, making it impossible to reach her. I stood up, knowing that I would not know. This child would remain closed. I backed up and crossed the threshold into the scrub room silently, worried that even noise might cause her further bruising. I took a breath and began to wash again.

Within four days of arriving, Debbie's illness overtook her body. Bruises arose on every limb; her skin became yellow-grey underneath each black-blue stain. She stopped eating or talking to anyone but her mother. Jackie and I met regularly over those days, and our work together became focused upon helping her realize that her daughter would not be healed. We held hands often, and once I showed her how to warm her hands by rubbing them together, then placing them on her own temples or stomach to ease pain. On the fifth day, Jackie asked permission to take her daughter home to die. Debbie had not opened her eyes in twenty hours and had stopped talking altogether.

The following morning, Jackie and I stood on either side of Debbie's portable bed. We had wheeled her into the hall and were waiting for the orderlies to let us know when the ambulance had arrived to take them to the airport. Jackie was holding Debbie's hand and I placed my hand on the small of Jackie's back. On the blanket near Debbie's face lay her horses.

"Hey, where the hell have you been, I've been calling for you." Marianna's voice resounded like steel on stone.

"Marianna. I'll be with you shortly. Why don't you wait in the conference room? I'm just waiting to say good-bye here."

"Don't shush me. Who's that?"

Marianna nudged her body behind me to stand next to Debbie's bed, saying a gruff "hi" to Jackie.

"Hey, you're the horse girl," she said to Debbie. "I heard about you."

I moved in between Marianna and the bed, preparing to move her down the hall, when I saw Debbie's eyes open. Jackie sucked her breath in, as surprised as I was.

"You're the horse girl; that's cool. Are ya leaving?"

"Debbie's going home, Marianna. This is a private moment; I'm sure Debbie wants to be alone with her mom." I could feel the sweat beading on my brow and under my arms.

I turned to Jackie. "I'm sorry, Jackie. I'll get a nurse . . ." Before I could finish, a soft voice cut through.

"Yeah, I'm going home." Debbie's voice was slow and soft, as if the words were making their way through a long, dense tunnel.

Marianna snorted. "I keep leaving and coming back. When you coming back?"

"I'm not." Debbie was looking directly at Marianna now. Jackie and I had moved closer to watch.

"How come?" Marianna had picked up the velveteen horse.

Debbie closed her eyes.

"You're all done?"

Debbie nodded.

"That sucks. Can I have one of your horses?"

"Marianna," I said, appalled. I reached to move her away when Jackie held my arm back.

"Okay," Debbie whispered.

"Which one you gonna give me? How about that brown-and-white one?"

Debbie nodded yes, and Marianna grabbed the horse, laying it on her shoulder as you would a small pet.

"Wanna know what I'm gonna do with it?"

Jackie and I stared at Marianna, transfixed by her boldness.

"I'm gonna take it home if they ever let me outta here, and I'm gonna give it to my friend Candy. She loves horses. Carries them around with her all the time. If you piss her off she starts whinnying like a horse. Drives me crazy. You do that, too?"

Debbie's shoulders shrugged.

"Candy'll keep this one, and that way you'll know somebody's taking good care of it."

Underneath the blanket, Debbie moved her arms to push her other horses off the bed. "Here, take them all."

"Naw, I don't want 'em. It ain't right." Marianna stepped back, crisscrossing her hands in front of her face.

"What do you mean?" Jackie asked.

"When you love somethin' it's good to hold on to it. Helps you feel like you're yourself, not somebody fuckin' else. Know what I mean, shrink?" Marianna leaned in to put her face an inch from mine.

I nodded, gently moving her face away.

"What's your name?" Marianna bent down now, her face close to Debbie's.

"Debbie." A whisper we could barely hear.

"Debbie Horse Girl. That's what I'll tell Candy. You're Debbie Horse Girl, cool?" Marianna put her hand out as if to shake Debbie's. When no movement came, she let her hand drop and straightened up.

"Okay, Debbie Horse Girl, okay?"

Debbie's head tilted, her chin pointed toward the ceiling, looking perhaps for an answer there. "Okay," came a moment later.

"Alright, then. Good-bye, Debbie Horse Girl." Marianna lifted the corner of Debbie's blanket and tucked her remaining horses under, hiding them completely. "Don't want them falling out now, right?" Kissing the air in front of my face, Marianna spun and pushed the elevator button four times with the brown-and-white's foreleg. "Damn elevators. So slow in this fucking place. They make 'em all for old folks, know what I mean?" She turned to me and aimed the horse's tail at my face. "I'll see you later, shrink." She turned and walked to the nurses desk, scraping the horse's feet along the wall, yelling at the top of her lungs, "Get me outta here!"

When the elevator came, Jackie pulled the bed in and I guided its head. As the door closed, I could see Marianna, standing at the nurses desk, the horse, secure in her right hand, held against her forehead in a military salute.

*   *   *

Two days later, after we had both heard of Debbie's death, Marianna paged me. Together we wrapped the horse in tissue paper and sent it to her friend, Candy, in a padded manilla envelope. Marianna shoved a note into the bag for her friend and taunted me that I could not read it.

"I'm glad you're sending this to your friend. Maybe you can tell her about Debbie one day," I said.

"If we mail it today, when will she get it?" Marianna had the envelope under her arm, ready to walk out. She wanted to take it to the mailroom herself, in the basement of the building adjacent to ours. I took it from her. She knew she wasn't allowed to leave the building.

"Two days, three at the most," I replied.

"Good. She should still be around by then."

"Is Candy in trouble?"

"We're all in trouble, shrink. You just never know who's gonna get hit by the next bus, know what I mean?" She grabbed the envelope from me, slammed the door behind her, and turned to press her face against the window glass, rubbing her tongue against the pane. Her saliva dripped to the bottom, and she laughed at the disgusted face I made. She skipped away and as I wiped up her mess, I laughed too. You just never know.

January 1997, four years later, my husband, Jonathan, began his first chemotherapy treatment for Hodgkin's lymphoma. Two weeks prior he watched his own chest x-ray slide out of the processing machine into his hands and noted a mass, the size of a small orange, settled between his right lung and his heart. Jonathan was anxious. As a neuroradiologist, he was precisely aware of the destructive potency of the drugs entering his system during chemotherapy treatments—AVBD, the "red poison" they called it in medical school. He told his doctor, Harvey, a long-time friend and colleague, that he could not sleep, could not quiet the litany of fears he had about the side effects and dying. Harvey nodded and smiled a wry smile. He had traveled this path with thousands. "Jonathan, I'm telling you, she [he pointed to me] will get hit by a bus long before you die of this cancer."

I went home that night and rewrote my life list. I want to grow old with my husband and my daughter. I want to play more hockey. I want to teach. I want to show my daughter the world—Italy or Boise (who knows what's there?). I want to remember that the death bus is always looming—and I want to never forget that the life bus is already here.

16
A Life That Counts

It was spring, mid-May, and I had been assigned Steven Hollister, a sixteen-year-old boy with aplastic anemia, a blood disease in which his bone marrow could not generate any of the normal blood lines: red cells, white cells, or platelets. His hair was brown, the color of wet sand. The skin of his extremely lean body was white with a purplish sheen. I could see within minutes of walking into the clinic room the bone count his ribs presented, the rim of his sternal notch, and each knuckle. Steven came monthly for blood transfusions. He apologized on our first visit three times while we awaited the bag's hanging, once to his mother for the strain this caused her, once to the nurse for his nausea at the smell of blood, and once to his younger brother, Thomas, for not being able to play catch the day before. They all appeared to smile easily at Steven and accepted his apologies without comment. I had a sense that his concern for others was not new.

"Do you collect baseball cards?" he asked, in response to my inquiry about how we might spend our time together. We were seated in a room with no window. In it was a weight scale, two cupboards, a sink, one visitor's chair, a doctor's swivel stool, two plastic bedpans, and framed pictures of blue, pink, green, and yellow swirls. It was large enough for three or four people to sit comfortably, yet somehow Steven's presence filled the space.

"No," I answered. "What else do you enjoy?"

"Nintendo, chess, anagrams, but none of those is possible here," he sighed.

"You could teach me chess, and anagrams are easy enough to find," I offered.

"No thank you, I can't concentrate when I'm here, it's too . . . well, tiring." He tilted his head toward the photos. "Artistic Muzak," he muttered. I remained still.

"What do you enjoy?" I watched him play with the hair at the back of his neck while we waited for blood to enter his body.

"Rocks, field hockey, poetry," I answered.

"Rocks," he repeated once, closed his eyes, and fell forward. He vomited on the floor, a green bilelike mucus, while I held his body to prevent him from falling over. I called his mother in to hold him. She whispered something in his ear while I wiped the floor. As I stood, Steven shook his head at me and I guessed correctly that he preferred to end our session for now. I informed his mom that I'd call the next day to check in and would plan to see Steven on his next visit.

Walking home that afternoon I had trouble thinking of anything but Steven. His disease, without radical changes in treatment, would kill him. And yet, to be in the room with him felt unusual and I wanted to try to understand

that. In the evening before sleep I sat quietly in meditation, remembering the entire twelve-minute visit and I
came to realize something: Steven was not afraid.

Prior to applying to graduate school I volunteered at the
New England Deaconess Hospital Mind/Body Clinic
in Boston. Known at the time as Herb Benson's or Joan
Borysenko's clinic, I worked there as a group assistant once
a week for two twelve-week sessions with approximately
twenty chronic-pain patients. These patients were adults,
predominantly in their forties, fifties, and sixties, who had
suffered for decades without relief. Many had had multiple surgeries and had tried up to fifteen different medications for back pain, migraines, stomach distress, nerve
sensitivity, and asthma. While the group leaders educated
our patients about the effects of stress and emotional distress on pain and the physiological connections between
thought and body, and guided them through imagery,
meditation, and introspection, I watched and supported
particular group members whenever necessary.

I remember very little from that time except something
that one female patient taught to another. We had been in
a small group discussion processing the week's lesson and
were intently listening to a woman in her late sixties who
had had chronic throat pain for nearly thirty years. Anna
woke regularly feeling as though her throat had nearly
closed and that her vocal cords and esophagus had
swollen. Her voice, a thin, high whisper, was almost impossible to hear, yet it seemed cruel to ask her to repeat

herself, since it appeared that speaking brought more pain. Physicians had tried various medications and surgeries with no success.

On this day, two-thirds through the group's training, Anna was crying. She had felt little improvement with the mind-body techniques and was frightened that her throat would never heal. One of the other group members reached out to help her; she may have actually walked over to Anna and crouched down in front of her to hold her hand. I remember only this: her caring voice telling Anna that positive change for her had not happened until she realized that fear of her chronic headaches brought more pain. When she became truly honest with herself, she learned that the fear was actually sometimes worse than the pain. She referenced a quote from Robert Frost's "A Servant to Servants"—"the best way out is always through"—and promised Anna she would stay connected with her if she was willing to face her fear as well as her pain. Through their connection, perhaps, she suggested Anna's fear would dissipate.

Despite his youth, Steven, like Lily, appeared to have crossed through this territory already to a place without fear.

In June I brought Steven my box, a white painted toolbox my father had made for me when I was nine. It held pebbles, river rock, quartz, agate, sea glass, and marble chips.

"I thought you could show me your baseball cards, and I could tell you about my rocks."

He placed the box on the sink stand and sat on the edge

of the bed, careful to tuck the johnny under each knee. He didn't actually need a johnny, but preferred not to endanger his own clothes with vomit. "No thank you, I only show my cards to people who can appreciate the game. I noticed that his arm bruises appeared larger than last month, or perhaps I simply had found the courage to look more closely. His file notes, which I had read in between our two visits, stated that it was unlikely he would live to be thirty.

" 'The Game,' capital *T*, capital *G*," I teased.

"The only one."

"Do you get to see any teams play?" I made a note in his file to ask about visiting baseball players. Jake's dad had mentioned seeing basketball players in the hospital signing autographs the previous spring.

Steven crossed his legs as the nurse entered.

"I'd rather you not stay," he told me.

I walked to the door. "Would you like your mom in the room?" He nodded yes, and asked the nurse for a blanket before she began hanging his new blood.

"Steven, I'll check in with you later."

Leaving the room, I found his mother, Julianne, reading a magazine in the clinic waiting area.

"Steven prefers that you stay with him. I think he doesn't want me to see him vomit again."

Julianne rose immediately and smiled fully. "Sixteen-year-old boys are sensitive about many things."

I smiled slightly. " I have a feeling he won't really benefit from talk therapy; he seems self-sufficient and grounded despite his disease."

"That's true." Julianne laughed. "I'm often not sure who is taking care of whom."

"Perhaps I could offer something different. A visit from a famous baseball player or a phone call at least."

"Now, that would be wonderful."

We spoke a few minutes more and I learned that Steven liked the Chicago Cubs and New York Yankees and hated the Boston Red Sox.

Two days later I called Steven at home to check on him. He was polite in replying to my questions, offering little more than was necessary in terms of response. I suggested that I could arrange a visit from a pro ballplayer if he would like and heard only his breathing on the other end of the line.

"Steven, are you okay?"

"I don't want to hurt your feelings, but I'd rather my parents take care of baseball for me. They really understand what I like."

"Steven, that's no problem, and you don't have to worry about hurting my feelings. I'm here to support you in whatever you need."

"Okay, then I'd rather not have a psychologist. I'd rather just do it how I did it before." I could hear his mother vacuuming in the background and imagined him in some favorite shirt, comfortable on a couch or lying back on his bed fully at ease. Next to his name on his chart I drew a star and another and another.

"Steven, thanks for telling me. I'll make sure your mom has my beeper number just in case you should ever want someone else to talk to."

"Is this okay? You aren't going to get in trouble with your boss, are you?"

"It's great, Steven." I sketched smiley faces inside the stars. "It's one of the best things a therapist can hope for."

"What?"

"That a child or an adult be surrounded by what he needs in the world and inside himself."

The vacuuming had stopped and I could hear country music playing in the background. Conor came to mind then—his passion for baseball as powerful as Steven's.

"Hey, Steven, before we say good-bye, do you mind one more question?"

"No, sure, that's fine." He was moving now, his sneakers squeaking on a smooth floor.

"I will meet other boys who love the game and sometimes it helps them to know that older boys like them have been in the hospital and have been okay," I flipped his file to the back cover, clear of any markings. "Is there anything you can think of to tell them, that might help them along the way? Anything you wish an older boy had been there to tell you when you began your treatments?"

The squeaking walk stopped. "I'm not sure, Maria. I'm not sure if anything would help. You just have to get through it."

Alright, I thought, time to let go. I thanked Steven for his truthfulness and wished him well. We hung up and I drafted a note to Donna explaining Steven's choice to discontinue therapy. A few hours later, on the way to supervision to review my cases, my beeper rang. It was Steven's home number and I dialed it from Donna's office.

"Maria, I had one thought for those other boys." His house was quiet now behind him.

"I'm listening, Steven."

"Just tell them that every day counts. Even if it's a sick day it still counts."

I could hear his mother whispering to him.

He continued. "What I mean is to try and find something that will make each day special."

"Even if they are sick that day," I repeated.

"Yes." I could imagine him nodding with a serious expression on his face. "Even if it's a bad day."

"I'll tell them, Steven. I'll remember what you said, and I'll make sure to tell the other boys I meet."

"Okay then, good-bye."

After we hung up. I added Steven's words to his chart and wrote them in my datebook: *Even if it's a sick day it counts.*

It is 1999. Three women, Barbara Viniar, Christine DeGregorio, and Naomi Gelfand, and I have cofounded a women's storytelling conference. Created to remind all of us that we are already unique and important, 150 women and men have come to spend a day participating in workshops in voice, drama, writing, weaving, introspection, and dance. It is the end of the day, the closing session, and I am asking our audience to share with us what they have learned that day. A young woman, a mother of two small boys, tells us that each night she struggles to tell her boys a grand fantasy story. It has to have adventure and dragons and talking animals, and there has to be a good guy and a bad guy and bad things have to be overcome and late in the day she begins to dread bedtime because she knows it will be exhausting to try to make up yet another incredible tale. Now, at the end of this day, she knows one thing: Her life, her story, and the stories of her boys' lives are all she needs. She now understands that she doesn't need to bring fantasy to her sons. It is enough to bring herself to them as she is and to bring their own quirky histories back to them. As young as they are, their life stories already have meaning and power. She will start with a diaper story, or a high-chair story, or some other simple moment that was real and true and unique to them.

Every day counts. Even if it's a bad day it counts. Even if your life is full of blood that does not heal itself, or chronic pain, or a heart that cannot keep its own rhythm, it is still your life and it still counts.

17
The Big Op

Peggy, a nurses' aide, stood directly in front of me in the elevator. To my left in the opposite corner stood a doctor I had not met, a bald, thin man with an oversized ribcage. I had sequestered myself in the back right corner in an attempt to get one more poem read before reaching the twelfth floor. It was May 5. Jason had given me a collection of Mary Oliver's poetry over the weekend, and I could not put down the book. Since Conor's death I had begun to read voraciously, seeking words from others to ground myself. This morning I was memorizing Oliver's "In Blackwater Woods." I closed my eyes, whispering to myself with the book hidden under my datebook, "To live in this world you must be able to do three things: to love what is mortal . . ." when Doc Ribcage let out a shriek, slammed his fists onto the elevator door, and screamed, "Not this time," kicking the door with his right foot on each syllable. Peggy jumped back, jamming me into the rear wall, her elbow crushing my shoulder and causing me to jerk away, which threw her off balance and onto the floor, where she dropped the linens she had been carrying. I screamed, "What the hell was that?"

Doc Ribcage looked at me, said, "Ninth floor," stepped over Peggy, and exited onto the tenth.

"This place is a looney bin," Peggy said as I lifted her to her feet.

"What was that?" I demanded.

"You don't know Dr. Pressman?"

"No, you do?"

"I forgot about how nuts he is. I would have waited for the next elevator."

I began to brush the carpet dust off Peggy's back. "What are you talking about?" We had stepped off onto twelve but I wasn't going anywhere until I knew what had just happened.

"Dr. Pressman is superstitious, he thinks the ninth floor is evil and won't ever get off there."

"What's on nine?"

"Administration."

"So how come he screams?"

"He thinks if he pounds the door and shrieks, the evil spirits won't enter the elevator."

"We have medication for people like him."

Peggy laughed. "The kids love him, so the doctors put up with him."

"Does he shriek in front of the kids?"

"I've heard he teaches them to howl like wolves when they get their IVs."

"Because . . . ?"

"Because it helps bring wolf spirit to the soul, which is supposed to help them fight."

"And they let him get away with this?"

Peggy smiled at me. "Supposedly his kids live."

"Who are his kids?"

"The bleeders."

Bleeders is an old, colloquial term for children with blood disorders; Pressman was a coagulation expert.

Peggy moved right and I headed down the corridor to orthopedic surgery, wondering if wolf calls could help my kids.

Gwen Bryant was waiting for me at the entrance to the surgical wing. A client of mine for three weeks, she made friends easily and signaled her joy at my approach by running over and hugging me around the waist. She released me abruptly and offered a crayon drawing: three bluebirds darting around a purple pool with yellow and pink stars marking the rim. The middle bluebird wore a single turquoise bead around her neck, as did Gwen.

Gwen and I had a hopping date. She had just met with her surgeon for the last time prior to her leg amputation, courtesy of an osteosarcoma, scheduled for the following week.

In her words, Gwen Bryant was seven and seven-eighths years old. That day she wore an orange and pink cotton shirt with short puffed sleeves. Her pants were blue corduroy with pink piping around the pockets. In each pocket, she had stuffed hidden treasure. A rock for her brother sat deep in her right pocket, placed there with the following commentary, "He's only three, so he might eat the rock, so I'll have to keep it in my room until he's old enough to know how to play with it." The left pocket held a tiny cloth figure, a worry doll given by a relative when Gwen was told she'd lose part of one leg to her bone tumor. She had showed me the doll for a brief second on our third visit, certain that it worked better if it stayed out of sight.

She wore white sneakers, dirtied at the toe as she used them as brakes for her two-wheeler. I knew this because her father, Will, had joked with her during our initial meeting that he'd save money now, only having to buy her one sneaker at a time. She had thought about this comment for a moment, then told him she would think of other things he could buy her with the money he saved on sneakers. I remember asking her what she would like him to buy her, wondering what might help someone adjust to losing a leg. But that was me. I might have been crushed, but not Gwen. "I'm gonna think about that one, but trust me," she turned to her dad, "it's not gonna be cheap."

This day Gwen wanted to hop to the river. We took the rear elevator to the ground floor after I determined that Dr. Pressman was not nearby. Turning left off of Binney Street, we walked the two blocks to the crossroads of the Riverway. Here we had three crosswalks to choose from, one cutting diagonally across the heart of the intersection or two which ran perpendicular across the four-lane Riverway. I asked Gwen which way she wanted to go.

"Which way gives us the longest hopping?" she asked.

"That way, the diagonal," I responded. And off we went. We practiced each session hopping on one foot and were both getting decent at it. On the other side of the Riverway, we hopped twelve hops to a staircase marked by two stone walls and a railing painted deep green.

"This railing is hard to see," she commented.

"How come, you think?"

"Because it matches the trees." She had noticed the stands of pine and spruce that lined the high hills behind the riverwalk path we were entering.

"Do you think the architect planned it that way, so that it would be sort of hidden?"

"Nah," Gwen said. "It was probably the only color they had on sale at the store that day."

This was classic Gwen, practical and unencumbered by the larger implications of action in the adult world.

At four feet, one inch, Gwen was an excellent hopper. She trained often, mostly on her left leg, which was the one that would remain intact. The Riverway that day was littered with small stones and pinecones. Gwen decided that we had to hop to a far maple, twenty yards away, without hopping on any stones. If we touched one we had to go back to the stairs. I complained.

"My feet are bigger than yours. There are millions of rocks here."

"Good," she said. "That means I'm gonna win."

She took off easily. After twelve hops or so she was back at the line, having broken the rule. I had only completed three hops and was holding steady, planning my strategy.

I saw no space large enough for a size seven heel to come down clearly. I was determined to check out all my options. Heading out again, Gwen stopped near me. Her brown hair, combed into one neat shoulder-length ponytail, had begun to escape its band. As she brushed it behind her ears I could see her gray-blue eyes clearly; they were squinting a bit, concentrating.

"It's no good if you give up so soon," she said. She hopped past, both arms out parallel to the ground. "I'm winning, I'm winning," she chanted.

"I'm not giving up," I countered. "I'm thinking my way out."

Gwen reached the maple easily this time and turned to wait for me. After my fourth failed attempt, I gave up and walked to join her.

"What's going to happen?" She had begun to throw stones into the river.

I wasn't sure what she meant.

"What's going to happen, Maria?" she repeated.

"You mean now?"

"No, I mean to my leg, the one the doctor takes off."

"I'm not sure." This was a new one for me.

"Can I have it?"

"Can you have your leg?"

"Yeah, I want to take it home. It's mine, you know?" She was right.

"I don't know, Gwen. I don't know if the doctors need to study it some more."

"I want it. It's mine and I want to bring it home." She

had stopped throwing stones to take my hand and pull me to sit.

"What would you do with it?" I was imagining her telling her parents she needed to sleep with her leg next to her favorite doll.

"I'd do the right thing." At this, Gwen scooted onto my lap sideways in order to twist my hair into braids. She hand-combed my hair first, then separated the left side into four small sections. According to Gwen she had invented this form of braiding. She and her older sister, Fiona, nicknamed it the Bryant Four Braid Weave. As she wove finger and hair under and over I leaned back to watch the river.

"What do you mean?" I asked, hoping to get at what Gwen was really saying.

"I'd give it a proper burial. That's what we called it at school when our guinea pig, Peanut Butter, died last year. Mrs. Cataldo said we had to give it a proper burial."

"How do you do that?"

"Well, you wrap the guinea pig up in a towel, and you put it in a box that all the kids decorate. I painted a sandwich, 'cause she was Peanut Butter, you know." She turned my face in her hands so that I would look at her directly, to see if I followed her logic. "Then we covered the box with tissue paper and ribbons, 'cause she liked to chew them even though they weren't good for her. We sang some songs, and then we put her in a hole next to the big swingset. Linda brought some flowers to put on the hole."

"So when you swing now, you can say hello to Peanut

Butter," I said. Visions of a funeral for a leg in the medical quad came to mind. A small cemetery for body parts could be created over in the corner by the nursing school. I was confident the nurses would understand.

"No, you can't say hello to her 'cause she's dead, but I can look at her spot."

I looked chagrined.

She shifted to braid the other half of my hair, raising my hand to hold the completed strand. "I have to do the other side now, for balance," Gwen continued. "I can still swing even after they take my leg."

"Yes, you'll be able to do mostly everything you can do now. Once you get your artificial . . ."

"So can I have it?" she interrupted.

"You want your leg so you can say good-bye to it properly, is that right?"

Gwen nodded.

"I'll find out for you." In my head I could hear Oliver's poem, "to hold it against your bones . . . and when the time comes to let it go . . ."

Gwen noticed my wet eyes.

"Maria, you are crying?"

"A little. It's true."

She let go of the braid to offer me her sleeve. "It's okay to lose. We can play again and maybe you'll win next time. I'll even give you a head start."

"I'm not sad because of losing. I'm just feeling lots of feelings, and one of them is how glad I am to know you."

"Adults are silly." She smiled at me. "Let's hop back fast and see how many it takes."

We race-hopped back. As we got close to the railing, Gwen reached back to take my hand. "You aren't going to win this time either, but you can tie with me."

We tied, holding hands, and started the climb up.

"Twenty-four stairs. Twenty-four will seem like a lot at first but then I'll get used to it. My mom says I'll get used to it and then it will seem like I always never had two legs."

"Right."

We held hands across the crosswalk, choosing the short path this time, and walking easily. The Bryants were waiting for us at the hospital entrance.

Her mom, Beth, brushed Gwen's hair back. "Have a good visit, Gwen?" she asked, looking at me above her daughter's head.

I nodded, smiling, while Gwen answered. "It was okay. I'm a hopper champion; she's still not so good."

"You're the best." Her dad, Will, grabbed her and swung her high.

"Gwen would like me to ask the surgeon if she can have her leg . . ." I began.

"Yeah, so I can bury it like Peanut Butter!"

Her parents looked surprised but intrigued.

"Is that customary, for a child to be able to bring her amputation home?" her mom asked, while Will shook his head.

"They probably need the leg to do research, Gwen," Will said. He had her up on his shoulder now, balancing her with one hand, while she mussed his hair.

"What's research?" Gwen asked, leaning over to look at her father, upside-down, face to face.

"Well, if they study your leg and find out how the cancer got inside there, maybe it will help prevent other children from getting the same kind of cancer."

"Oh." Gwen kept silent for a moment. I could see her stretching for the secret rock in her pocket. She swung herself down.

"Maybe the kid before me took her leg home and didn't let the doctors study it and that's why I got cancer."

"Maybe . . ." I offered, "or maybe sometimes cancer just happens."

"Well, you'll find out for me, right? It's my leg."

"If you can't have the leg back," I said, "we can still find a way to say good-bye to it properly."

Gwen grabbed her parents' hands and tilted her head down. "I'll have to think about that."

"Perhaps you and your folks can think about it together until we see each other for the surgery."

Will nodded. "I'm sure we'll come up with some options, huh, Gwen?"

"Yup, Dad. Bye Maria. See you next week for the Big Op."

"Big Op?"

"That's what Fiona and her friends call it. She says it's cool."

"The Big Op it is, then."

We blew kisses at each other and Gwen left, swinging herself between her parents, lifting herself into the air with every third step, ready to take on the world and hold it close, against her bones—and prepared, more than most, to figure out just how and when to let it go.

18
Freedom

Ten o'clock the next morning I was headed to my office, only to be grabbed by a pediatric nurse, Jeanine, who said, "Page Josie. She has to speak with you immediately."

"I'll head over to BMT. Maybe one of the kids is in trouble."

On BMT, three nurses were gathered at the station while Dave, the head of security, consulted with Catherine. Josie pulled me aside, tapping her pen against her stethoscope. Marianna could not be found. She had gone AWOL from her room and had not been seen for nearly an hour. We divided up the hallways and floors and began to check each patient room, bathroom, and storage room. For two hours we searched, to no avail.

"She told me she'd rather die on the street," Josie said, shadowing me as I inspected the floor, room by room.

"What started this?"

Josie shook her head, "Who knows, Maria? She was in her room watching TV when the resident went in to prep her. The next thing I know, they are screaming at each other. I went to page you, and by the time I made it back she was gone."

"What were they screaming about?"

"She wouldn't let anyone clean her line."

"Were you direct with her? Did you try to snow her? She hates that."

"Maria, she hates most interactions. It wasn't anyone's fault. She just blew."

We finished the search. No child had seen her, nor had any parent. She was either hiding out on another floor, in a storage room somewhere, or had left the building.

"I need to call her aunt and uncle and then I'll page Donna and check in with security in the other buildings to see if she's shown up in some other part of the complex." I left Josie and headed over to my office.

Before calling Donna I decided to speak to the security staff in the lobby to make sure they knew who Marianna was and where to bring her should she appear. The elevator was up on twelve. Too impatient to wait, I used the outer stairwell down, taking the steps two at a time. On the second floor landing, I caught sight of the smokers on break gathered under the hospital's entryway overhang. They were hooting, an unusual sound at the hospital. I stopped to look and saw Marianna wearing a johnny, jeans, and a torn leather jacket, cigarette burning and smoke circling as she kissed her middle finger, then flipped the bird to each passerby.

I had the security guards escort her to my office, not wanting to engage her with a crowd at her disposal.

She stepped into my office, leaned against the doorjamb,

and threw her jacket onto my desk, her cigarette cupped in her hand.

"Throw it away, Marianna. What were you thinking?"

"What are you going to do about it?"

"Marianna, tell me what happened." She flipped me the bird then and took her cigarette over to the window, smashing it on the sill.

"Nothing happened, babe, nothing you need to get all excited about." Her back to me, she unwrapped the paper, allowing the tobacco to fall. She took the filter between two fingernails and shredded it onto my floor. I chose to watch this without comment, knowing that any conflict could set her off. Cigarette trash could be vacuumed; her cooperation was much more important.

"Josie tells me you don't want to have the porta-cath cleaned."

She mocked me, dropping her head from side to side like a puppet on a loose wire.

"Marianna, you need the line for the meds."

"Not if I don't have the transplant."

"Marianna, you don't have a choice. You know that." Her transplant was scheduled for the next day.

"Fuck you, fuck you! I'm not letting you cut me up. Fuck you." She jumped up on my desk then threw my papers onto the floor, all the while yelling to be let out. I shut the door and pulled the chair out of her reach so it could not be thrown. I tried to grab her arms, but she jumped from desk to desk, kicking papers, books, phones onto the floor. On the last desk, Jason's, she found a glass paperweight that she began banging against her head while reciting in singsong, "Not gonna go, it's gonna snow, not gonna go, it's gonna snow."

"Marianna, you must stop. You're going to hurt yourself." I reached for the paperweight while pulling her to sit. She laughed at me and stopped herself, handing over the paperweight, only to grab a letter opener. She put it next to her eye, daring me to try to take it away.

"You are scaring me. That will hurt you." I put my body directly in front of hers so she could see me clearly and be reminded that another human being was in the room.

"Marianna, look at me. Please tell me what is going on." She brought the letter opener down, level to the well underneath my eye. I slowly put my hand on top of hers and lowered the point. I took it from her grasp and threw it toward the opposite desk, where it glanced against the wall, scarring the paint. The white gash it left against the pastel paint surprised us both. She sat down on Jason's desk, her right hand pulling hair out of her head, one strand at a time. I watched as she let each hair dangle from her hand before leting it go to settle onto my face, long black strands decorating me, like a web or a shroud.

I let her cover me, knowing in some way she was showing me a pain she was unable to talk about. Minutes passed, perhaps five or six, and she stopped, her body slumped, and she cradled her head in her arms.

"Marianna, you're scared," I said softly. "I'm scared for you. Bone marrow is big, really big."

"You'll need to drug me, Maria. I'm not going on my own."

"What happened, Marianna? What upset you?"

"They told me. It's gonna happen to me."

"What were you told?" I moved to sit next to her and could see now the cuts along her arms, thin surface scratches pointing like arrows to her throat. When had she done these?

"That boy died."

"Who?"

"That boy. The baseball kid, he died."

"Conor, yes, he did. I'm sorry. I didn't realize you knew him. He died a few months ago, before Christmas." I wondered where this was going.

"I didn't know him. So what?"

She was right. What difference did that make?

"And Debbie Horse Girl."

"Yes, she died, too." I sat as near as I could, so she could feel the warmth of my skin, reaffirming my presence and the reality of our two bodies next to each other.

"And Stacey."

"Stacey isn't going to make it to bone marrow."

"Exactly. You are batting zero in here as far as I can tell. New marrow means shit."

"And?"

"So why can't I die how I want, out there, on the street with my friends?"

"Marianna, he died. She died. It doesn't mean you will."

"Fuck you, doesn't mean that I won't, now does it?"

I wanted to massage her shoulders, rub her hands, will her to feel her body, to remember its force.

"Marianna, whatever you need to get through this, I'll

try to get for you. But I can't just let you disappear to die on the streets. Bone marrow may kill you, but it may kill the cancer and the streets can't do that. You'll die in pain out there."

"I already have pain and it's gonna get worse."

I knew then that I was up against a wall. Words don't always help. Therapy, rooted in language and conversation, only offers so much. Marianna knew I couldn't guarantee her life or painlessness. I could promise nothing. I moved my eyes toward her head and imagined myself stroking her hair gently, as a mother might a young child. I mapped in my mind the shape of her skull, let it tell me where to press and where to lift, wished my love into her bone, and kept silent until the words could come true.

"Marianna, I don't want this body to die. Let's find a way to not let it die."

She sat up and pushed my face toward the window. I stared out and watched city pigeons land on the concrete near the Au Bon Pain across the street, where the nurses and residents were congregating to drink coffee and plan their days.

"I don't want to know what you are doing," she said. "I don't want to feel it anymore." She got up and walked out, her resignation palpable. I turned to pick up her jacket and cover her but she had gone. I paged security and had them find her at the elevators and escort her back to BMT.

After consulting with her Aunt Joanie and Uncle Paul, we began Marianna on a course of antianxiety medication for twenty-four hours, just long enough to get her to transplant. The surgery went smoothly. Marianna recuperated over the course of five weeks in BMT. She refused to see me during that time, though I checked on her daily. Whenever possible we continued the anxiety medication, keeping her quiet and complacent, and on some days, ignorant of her body's struggle to heal.

Throughout her stay she allowed the nurses and physicians to examine her without putting up a fight, which was odd and unsettling. She answered few questions and left cards unopened. Her aunt and uncle asked me to either assign someone else to Marianna's case or force myself into her room. But I knew that would be foolish and counterproductive. Marianna was done with care. Her anger had been a doorway, an invitation to engage with her, albeit on difficult terms. Stilled into passivity at the end of medicine's attempts to heal, Marianna wanted no more from us. Six weeks posttransplant Marianna went home. She refused to answer my calls or return to the hospital for checkups. One month later she left her aunt's house. It was a Wednesday evening, two days before her eighteenth birthday. She grabbed her backpack, stuffed her aunt's wallet and a few music tapes into it, Pink Floyd and Aerosmith, and left. Joanie chose not to pursue her or the wallet. Marianna was gone, without a trace, free to die as she chose. She was eighteen and none of us could manage her life any longer.

19
Stacey

Three weeks had passed since Marianna's bone marrow transplant. I woke on a wet, windy June morning to the sound of cawing crows and barking dogs. Gwen survived her surgery beautifully and the next day, Monday, I would see her for our first hopping rematch without her leg. In two months she'd begin wearing her prosthesis. We planned to see each other two more times, assuming that her cancer-free status held.

I huddled in bed, a white summer-weight down comforter covered my bent knees as I half-listened to the *Car Talk* guys on National Public Radio tease a woman about buying her ex-husband's used car. A coffee mug with bald children sketched in a dancing circle warmed my hands. Above the children, in rainbow-colored letters, the cup read, YOUR BEST FRIENDS NEVER TELL YOU THERE'S SOMETHING WRONG WITH YOUR HAIR. Jake, returning to the hospital in May for a checkup, brought it to me as a present. It sat on my nightstand each night with water and in the mornings I filled it with tea. But that morning I thought about neither Gwen nor Jake, but about the end of the year and Stacey.

Some children we appreciate; some we love and wish we could carry home and raise; and some inhabit us, settle in our marrow, take root with vine and blossom and live there, entwined, where it is dark and secret and quiet. Such a child was Stacey.

Stacey was sixteen that year. Blond streaks ran through her now-thin brown hair, and she dressed funky and sloppy. Sandy tells me that in the early days, when Stacey's father accompanied her to the hospital she wore white blouses and tailored pants with matching sweaters. Now, her third ear piercing often held something sacreligious, like an image of the pope crucified on a large silver cross. She wore fifteen silver bangles on her wrist and complained about taking them off every time we checked her. She never came to the hospital without her Walkman on and would only let her resident, Scott, know what she was listening to. She and Scott had a thing, a mild flirtation, which sometimes happens between patients and doctors, especially when the stakes are high and nothing is working. None of us minded. We were glad for any moments of pleasure she had, and relieved that some part of her worked like a normal teenager. Her diagnosis of Hodgkin's lymphoma at age twelve had taken away most of the normalcy in her life.

I was asked to help Stacey through her final year. That was the assigned task on her chart, which had been given to me by Donna nine months earlier. I was new enough to the service then that the term *final year* still held possibility so I naïvely asked Donna what she meant. "Does this mean final year of treatment or final year of stay here or final year of life?"

Donna looked at me with compassion, which I had yet to learn could be a bad sign at a cancer hospital. "Final year of life, Maria. She's not expected to live much longer."

"Oh." I went down to the pediatric floor to meet Stacey, file in hand, unread.

When I went into the clinic's waiting room she sat with her back to me, leaning toward the window, with her Walkman on high enough that I could hear the music, REM, eight paces back. I sat across from her, smoothing my orange and lavender linen skirt.

"Jesus, turn it down, lady," Stacey said, shielding her eyes from my skirt's brightness.

"Too much?"

"Way too much, and you aren't supposed to wear linen after Labor Day."

"But I like linen," I responded. "Some of those rules are old news, don't you think?" I wondered where she put herself on the independence spectrum.

"Sometimes the rules make sense," she countered.

"How about here?"

"I like this."

"You like talking like this?"

"I like no bullshit. Let's go for a walk."

Stacey and I walked outside that late September day, her steps slowed by pain in her joints. She insisted on crossing over to the Simmons College lawn, a good ten blocks away, taking the longest possible path to maximize her time out of the hospital. Every few paces she rested, giving nurses and doctors on their way past a chance to stop and embrace her. Stacey was a veteran here and well liked, that was clear, but something else was present in the greetings exchanged. They reminded me of hugs from my grandmothers, hugs that squeezed, softened, then ended with a clear, straight look into my eyes, a look that sought as well as offered.

I found myself reaching to grab her elbow but held back. At her age I had wanted no help and imagined she would be the same, cancer or not.

On that walk I learned much about her. Stacey liked Mexican food, but since radiation four years ago her esophagus burned when she ate spicy dishes. So she paced herself, choosing to eat out only when she had enough energy to suffer the next day. She preferred pop rock to all other kinds of music and kept the entire Little Women series on her nightstand at home. Her best friend had gotten laid at fifteen, but Stacey was still a virgin. She had hoped her junior prom would have yielded a "boy with an urge," in her words, but had let go of that fantasy as of her last failed treatment.

Stacey said she thought she was dying even though none of her docs had said so. I asked her how she knew. "My friends have stopped visiting, it's all too gloomy;

chemo and girl talk don't exactly mix," she told me that first day. "The whole dying thing is a bummer."

"How so?" I asked.

"No one can relate, like none of my friends get it and the folks who do, they're dying, too, and who wants to talk to them?"

I was impressed by her honesty but worried by it also.

"Some people think that those who are close to death hold wisdom," I said.

At this she laughed out loud and turned for the last loop back to the hospital. "That's therapist crap. I'm supposed to think that I have wisdom, that you would be desperate to talk to a teenager to learn something? Give it up."

"Okay, tell me straight why you don't want to talk to people who are dying, who can, as you say, relate to you better than anyone."

At this she stopped and put her hand on my arm, a grin crossing her face. "You don't know my story, do you?"

"Not yet."

She grinned at me, a know-it-all teenager grin. Her eyes narrowed and she turned away, leaning against my back briefly, then pushing off. She walked the last four paces to the door and held it open for me.

"You can't help me, Maria. It isn't going to matter if you learn it all or not."

At the clinic Bill took Stacey from me, chatting about her latest CD purchase, and led her into a treatment room. I looked for a parent or relative to check in with and schedule a follow-up session, but no one was around. I wondered if Stacey had driven herself to the clinic or had taken a cab. I decided to find a quiet spot to read her chart and took the elevator to the eighth floor medical library. In a pine cubby in the farthest westward corner, where I would least likely be disturbed, I opened her chart and read for nearly forty-five minutes.

Stacey had gone through four different chemo regimens, two radiation courses, and two experimental drug trials from Europe. After an initial hopeful response, her cancer returned each time. By her fourth year of care, Scott had begun to measure success by her stamina rather than the length of time she was without cancer. At this point, she was being monitored weekly to see how the cancer was progressing. Her treatment was palliative, though in Scott's most recent note written a week ago, he considered speaking to her father about bone marrow transplant as an option.

The medical notes ended there, which made no sense. It had been two weeks since Scott had considered BMT, and Stacey had been in the clinic last week. I searched through the file until I found the admission forms and social worker reports from Stacey's early years at the hospital. Stacey had been admitted in May 1989. She had been brought by her father, Tim. She reported having two stepsisters, both in college. Her mother had disappeared when Stacey was three; no one had had contact with the mother in the interim years.

The first psychology intern's notes followed. Stacey hated anything to do with traditional therapy; she wanted to simply hang out with the therapist and watch movies or talk about boys. Her friends visited regularly then, and she often chose to end therapy in order to have private time with Tina and April, her two buddies. The intern stated that her sisters did not visit that first year and had only called one time while Stacey was in house as an inpatient. For July 27, 1992, the note was four sentences long. It read: "Tim admitted to hospital today. Diagnosis, lung cancer with mets to the brain. Stacey is distraught. We cannot reach her sisters."

I stopped reading for a moment, remembering that no parent had been with Stacey in the clinic that morning.

The notes went on to record four years of remission and relapse and brief conversations with Tim, who had undergone brain surgery, radiation, and one round of chemo for his lungs. Stacey's first two psychology interns told stories of her courage, her belief that both she and her father would get better, and her fantasy that her sisters cared. A third psychology intern entered only two notes, reporting without explanation that she was transferring the case to Donna.

The final psychology note, written in August 1992 by Donna, two weeks before I began working at the cancer center, explained the attention shown by the staff during our morning walk. It stated simply:

> Stacey was informed today by Scott that her only hope would be BMT, even though she is not in re-mission. Her father will be receiving radiation with the goal of keeping his brain clear as long as possible.

His lung cancer thrives, tumors continue to reappear in his brain. It has become an unspoken challenge at the adult clinic to see if we can keep her father alive long enough to say goodbye to his daughter. We have given up hope of reaching her sisters and have begun to look for other relatives, given Tim's failing state. Stacey has begun to show signs of depression, specifically insomnia, restlessness, and little desire to eat. Her clinic visits have been increased; we will see her each week to monitor her status and determine when BMT may happen. Tim has been unable to speak coherently the past two weeks. Stacey requests that we hold off BMT until her father can help her recover. This may not happen.

I closed the file.

Nine months passed. Stacey spent most of this time in a private room, courtesy of the hospital. We found one relative, an aunt, Tim's sister, Kara, who lived across the country in Washington. She told us she would fly in "when the end comes." Stacey does not know her well and does not count on this. "Sisters suck," was her only comment. Tim had his own room on the adult wing.

Stacey and I listened to music, walked when she could, and talked, often about boys and sex, sometimes about college, never about her sisters or her mother. When he was able, Tim accompanied us, wheeled over by an orderly, which was not easy. Five foot eleven, he had no fat on his bones. His hair, formerly blond, had become a patchwork of brown stubble and scars. He suffered short-term memory loss, instability in his limbs, and a bizarre twist to his face on the left side. There were times on the floor when Tim began a visit normally, rubbing Stacey's head, holding her hand, offering the caring words a father sends from his heart. Then, in the time it took to turn a page, his face would shift, he'd lose his balance, and in only a few moments would forget that Stacey was his daughter and that they both were dying. In those moments it was hard to look at them. Stacey crumbled, begging her father to return. She yelled for Scott to come, to give Tim a shock treatment, a drug, anything to bring him back, and I stayed with her, a steady presence, until her rage passed. I learned to tell her the one thing that helped. "Stacey, I'm here. You aren't alone, I'll stay with you until he comes back." We'd wait, myself or the nurses, for minutes, sometimes hours, for the tumors to move enough to press on a different part of the brain, returning Tim to himself. Some days that did not happen.

By the end of July, Stacey had declined dramatically. Tim cascaded into deeper unrealities. He no longer remembered that he had a daughter. No doctor on either team had anything left to try.

On Friday, August 1, the pediatric oncology chief, Joshua Webber, paged me. He asked me to attend medical rounds the following Monday. In eleven months of working at the hospital I had never been asked to this meeting. I left work on Friday with trepidation, worried that I was to be reprimanded about a judgment call with which the medical team disagreed, yet in my heart I knew it would be about Stacey.

20
The Lines of the Living

It was 1970. I was ten years old. Behind Kay Tregaski's house were woods where pine and spruce met oak and willow. The branches entwined high and dense so that sky had no room, yet somehow it was light. The leaf and needle canopy sheltered moss-covered ground, which cradled granite block, fern, and rotted log. It was cool, too, and close. Silence nested there as did the creatures I loved: white butterflies, black ants, neon green caterpillars, and the anxious chipmunks I only ever saw from behind. There lived privacy and for a time, fairies. I would run to the woods always, leap and run to prepare the table for the Fairie Queen.

"Maria, where are you going?" my mother asked.

"Nowhere."

"Nowhere?"

"To my spot."

"Come home in an hour. The laundry will be done then and I'll need help with supper."

"Okay, Mom."

"Take your sweater."

"Ma-ommm."

"I don't want you kids to get sick; you know that."

"Okay, Mom, I'll get it."

When I got to the woods I hung the sweater on a maple's low branch and got to work. I gathered first the moss and cut nine small squares with a plastic knife. I set them in a semicircle, one palm-width between each square. In front of the nine "cushions" I laid a pebble for a footstool and to the right I anchored a twig, weapons should the maidens need to defend their queen. I ran then to the creek and washed my hands as the priests did, knelt at the bank, bent low, muttered song and prayer, and ran back to the woods, hands upraised to air-dry. At the circle's edge I stopped to call the queen to come, assuring her that all was well and nearly ready. Holding my right hand inches above the ferns, I concentrated to choose which fern would be the best. I thanked the fern and broke it gently at the root. With the frond I brushed the queen's seat, a large granite block. Run through with crystal, it shone and hummed. I encircled the granite throne with feathers: gray-brown goose, white-gray duckling, brown-gold turkey. These were my gift offerings and upon each I settled a marble or bead. I centered the pink teacups and saucers in front of the stone. This done, I sat to the left on a maple's rotted stump and waited, a silent vigil, until my mother's voice called me home.

August 1993. In twenty-four hours I was going to meet with Josh Webber. I headed to a local park where young adults gathered to sunbathe or study, mothers and fathers strolled, pushing their young children in carriages, and the elderly sat on green benches, sweaters buttoned high as they watched the activity around them. I brought a journal and a blanket and laid on my stomach in the middle of the widest patch of grass. "Stacey remains a virgin," I wrote at the top of a journal page, then turned the book over. I wanted to feel life rather than write about it.

In front of me, to the right, against a birch stand, two mothers with toddlers had spread a picnic blanket. On it were cheese, bread, grapes, olives, melon slices, juice boxes, an untouched *New York Times,* magnetic puzzle sets, a baby doll and stroller, a pad of construction paper, crayons and stencils, a stack of napkins weighted by a rock, and a mixed assortment of paper plates. One of the children, a girl, I guessed four years old, had light brown hair to her waist and I gave a silent cheer—one more for the yet-untouched-by-chemo side. Her younger brother, buckled into a stroller, drooled Cheerios, his feet circling as he placed one piece at a time onto his tongue. The mothers talked about sleep patterns and preschools. Their conversation was an oasis to me and I sent their children a mental wish – may their childhoods offer long days in private places where they too can feel some magic in the world.

To my left two college-age girls sunbathed in bikini tops and athletic shorts. Sunblock had replaced the baby oil of my youth and as they applied it in unison, each listened to her own Walkman, separate yet together. The smell of their lotion reminded me suddenly of the skin cream I wore the summer my cousin Tommy died and just as suddenly he was there with me, hovering above.

I turned away from the girls to face a distant field. High school boys played frisbee with a dog. A father knelt down in the grass with a small boy pointing, I imagined, to a ladybug or worm. A few old men and women sat on the benches that bordered the park's footpath and I tried to guess what my grandfather would have looked like in his eighties. I sat up and rested my upper body on my forearms, looking ahead at the park's small pond. White duck feathers edged its surface, but no ducks were evident that day. Were we not far enough south? Two women in their midfifties crossed in front of me, speaking quietly, and behind them a homeless woman shuffled. At eye level, her shoes appeared corroded, tan orthopedic walkers stained with tar or ash, ragged holes at each heel edged with black. Her legs, flaking and hairy, were unprotected; ripped socks without elastic puddled around her ankles. My childhood priest's words came to mind, "and there will be poor always," and I got it, right then: there will be poor always, there will be death always, the lives of the living will always carry the dead and the dying behind them.

I looked again and saw behind each person imaginary lines, those already dead and the soon-to-die. We carry our losses with us no matter where we go; it is foolish to believe otherwise. I swung back to the baby with his Cheerios and watched his happy feet dance as his mother held a plastic cup with juice to his mouth. "I'm with you, babe," I whispered. "Drink up while you can." I smiled at the family and waved even though we were unknown to each other, grateful and graced by their normalcy, their seemingly untouched lives.

21
Holding On

On Monday morning, at nine fifty-nine a.m., the pediatric oncology conference room was full. I scanned the group, my intuition confirmed. With the exception of the chief, Stacey's team was gathered.

"We will be stopping all treatment except pain management on Stacey Neale," Joshua said, leading off the discussion. "Hospice was informed over the weekend, as was the VNA. They have been given explicit instructions to offer her twenty-four-hour care. Tim Neale will be informed by his doctor this morning, though we do not anticipate comprehension on his part. All that is left is to tell Stacey that she is going home."

The room was silent.

Joshua turned to me. "Maria, you've worked with her for some time now. We think it's appropriate for you to tell her. We'd like her to be told today so that we can accelerate home care for her."

I sat, astonished. In every other case the chief resident, the doctor who had cared for the patient since admission, was the one to pass on this news. I swiveled to look at

Scott. He had been Stacey's physician and ally for over three years; we all knew he loved her. He was looking down at the papers in front of him, his hands folded on the pile. The room felt heavy, dense with sweat, though it was early in the day. I suddenly knew what was happening. Scott could not tell her, and I was being asked to fill in for him.

I nodded assent. Joshua and I spoke about the details, how she would get home, which team would be in charge of her care in the house, who would pack up her things, and I committed to see Stacey at eleven and tell her what she must know. As I left the room, Scott kept his face averted.

As chief resident he had seen close to fifty children die in his four years on the service. Our physicians face a daily onslaught of bad news, difficult decisions, anxious patients, and unpredictable outcomes, all under the intense pressure of not enough time and the internal desire to do it all right for each patient every time. Turn to any major international medical publication in the last four years and articles on physician fatigue, burnout, and stress abound. It is, in this new century, a profession that asks an extraordinary amount of its practitioners with little scaffolding to carry them through the emotional and mental exhaustion of the chronic presence of suffering. Sometimes it is simply too much to bear.

I paged Donna and asked for an emergency meeting. We talked about how to begin with Stacey, how to reassure her that she would not be alone when death finally came. We wrestled about whether to initiate questions of faith or afterlife or God. We both knew that Stacey deserved to control the content of her conversations; she had control over nothing else. Yet Donna listened as I thought out loud about introducing the topic to see if we could find a way to offer Stacey comfort. I couldn't justify it, though. Any desire I may have had about speaking of God or an afterlife was probably more about soothing my own anxiety than about easing hers. Donna agreed. It would be Stacey's choice to ask.

At eleven a nurse stood next to Stacey's bed, completing a temperature check. When I walked in she sent the nurse out immediately.

"What's going on? They've taken out my IVs, and I didn't get the usual meds with breakfast." She lifted both her arms so that I could see. I took her arms at the elbow and helped her sit up. According to her chart, she weighed 112 pounds, yet I knew I could have picked her up easily. I tilted her forward to adjust her pillows. She laid back, short moans coming as I adjusted her blanket. Her breasts slipped to the side of her johnny and lay long and flat, breasts more like those of an old woman than a teenager. A mole the size of a penny sat above her right elbow, and from it and through it and over her leg and belly and arm ran bulging purple-blue veins. Her lymph nodes were engorged, swelling her arms and her neck. Her head held scant hair. There was no part of her untouched by her disease.

"Stacey, I met with the medical team this morning. They are going to be coming by later to see you. Scott will be here at noon but you need to know something. There's nothing else the doctors can do for you with medicine. It's time to go home."

I attempted to cover her with a second blanket. She pushed it away, afraid of its weight.

"When can I see my dad?" Her straight-on gaze challenged me.

"I'll bring him over as soon as we're done."

"Does he know?" she asked. We both knew this was a moot question. She was like a child learning the truth about Santa Claus—anxious to know but not ready to take it in.

"He was told earlier this morning, but it's not clear that he remembers."

"I want to see him now. Please leave."

"Okay, sweetie. I'll check back later."

I told the nurse to have her dad brought over from the adult wing as soon as possible. I heard later that he greeted Stacey as a new friend, offering to shake her hand and help her move things to the elevator when it was time for her visit to end. Stacey screamed. Her nurses removed Tim and paged Scott. Scott remained with her for more than an hour. When he left the room, he carried her chart to the nurses station, took a blue ball point pen, and printed on its cover in capital letters, MANAGE HER PAIN.

Stacey chose not to see me that afternoon or the next day. Frantic that she would die without a chance to say good-bye, I spoke to her nurses every two hours, but remained firm in my belief that her time could only be hers to control.

On Thursday morning, the day she was to go home, she paged me.

The nurses had packed for her. The walls no longer held a month's worth of watercolor drawings, posters of rock groups—REM, Bon Jovi, KISS—and cards from her classmates, sent at Christmastime and New Year. Her suitcase sat zipped to the left of her bed. The room was strangely silent. Machines meant to measure heart rate, blood oxygenation, and temperature were gone.

"I'm here, Stacey." Her eyes were closed. I covered her hand with mine and moved a chair close to her bedside.

Her voice was a thin croak, a voice without moisture or strength. "I want to know something."

"Okay."

"I want to know what happens when I die. My father can't tell me. What do you know?"

I thought about the mysteries of the Catholic Church, about St. Peter and his gates, my grandmother's warnings about purgatory, essays on the Tibetan bardo, the Buddhist law of karma, Freud's writings about afterlife as illusion, Casteneda's Great Eagle. Stories I had read about life after death, near death experiences, the light or the ancestors coming, or the children who know angels all passed through my mind. I watched her breathing, shallow, harsh. I chose none of the stories for I could attest to none of them. To lie to this child would be abomination.

I told her that I had no answer for her about death's reality, that the one thing I could say for certain is that those who die live on in our memories.

"Who's going to do that for me?" Her eyes remained

closed. I focused there, on her eyelids, willing them to open for my sake.

"I will. I will remember you and the pictures you drew and how you dressed."

"Will you tell people about me?" Her voice was barely audible even in the silent room. I put my mouth near her ear and spoke as quietly as I could.

"We'll all talk about you here, Stacey; we won't stop talking about you. Scott and I will never see each other without thinking and talking about you." Below her still-closed eyes moisture appeared.

"But you're moving when the year's done, you told me, you won't be here to talk about me. You'll forget about me."

It was all I could do not to take her in my arms and hold her.

"Stacey, I will remember you until I join you in whatever there is after we die. I will not forget you." I stroked her hair tentatively, keeping my head angled away so that my tears did not fall onto her face.

I was aware that the hallway was quiet, even the hospital seemed muted. I reached for my pager and turned it off. Time had become short for both of us. In four days my work on pediatric oncology would end. New psychology interns had already been chosen, and most of my clients had been transferred to them. I had said good-bye to many of the children. Ninety-six hours would bring a new life to me. For Stacey, cancer had effectively stopped the clock. She would not even have four days left.

It was impossible to leave her. I crossed over to the phone on her nightstand and left Donna a message that I would remain with Stacey until her Aunt Kara arrived. Tiptoeing around her bed, I pulled my chair closer and laid one hand on her head and one hand over her hand. She curled her fingers into my palm, my hand enveloping hers. We were both holding on.

Forty minutes later, Kara arrived, and Sandy, Scott, Kara, and I wheeled Stacey down. Her father, lost to himself, remained in his hospital bed, unaware of his daughter's last ride. An ambulance met us in the parking garage; two medics transferred Stacey and drove her and her aunt home. The hospice team met Stacey at home and began a twenty-four-hour watch.

I walked the halls of the hospital, incapable of work, though I continued. I prepped a five-year-old for an upcoming transplant, played checkers with an eight-year-old with leukemia, and finished my notes on yesterday's sessions. I called Stacey's home two hours after she had left the hospital and was told that she was already in a coma-like state, unbreachable.

I phoned that evening again at dinnertime and spoke to the nurse and Kara. Stacey's hands were cold, Kara told me, locked like bird claws frozen to a branch. I asked Kara if I could come to the house, if she thought it would be helpful. She said no, Stacey was too far gone to know and the nurses had been great. Not ready to end, I asked Kara to describe what Stacey's bed looked like so I could imagine her clearly. She told me this: In a hospital bed in the living room Stacey was covered by a quilt given her when she was seven by her father. It was sewn with swirls and stars in lavender, black, blue, silver, and white, a magician's cloth. Her journal lay near her, as did a stuffed animal given to her by her grandmother when she turned three. Kara recognized the bear, having helped her mother choose it for Stacey thirteen years earlier. It was a koala of light brown patched hair, with a single black string left for a nose. I thanked Kara for her words and begged her to call if anything was needed.

22
Stones

The woods bordering Arlington's western border were mostly evergreen stands. Blue spruce, balsam, and pine, reaching fifteen feet into the air, brought smells I associated with Christmas and childhood. After hanging up from Kara, I left my apartment, instinct propelling me to the forest. I walked the woods, holding my hockey stick, a crimson-wrapped Dita, loosely in my right hand, like a hiker's staff, to move aside leaves, small branches, and rocks. Near a dried streambed, I found a piece of rose quartz. I picked it up and glanced down the bed to see four cairns, piles of rocks balanced upon each other to form one- to two-foot-high pyramids. I entered the streambed and walked along slowly, discovering other pieces of quartz scattered here and there among gray stone and granite. As I approached the cairns, I noticed rose and amethyst quartz placed between the dull native stones. The town's girls and boys must have made other cairns over time that had fallen down, which explained the pink and purple stones cast along the streambed.

I gathered ten quartz pieces and laid each one next to the other, alternating rose and amethyst with native black and gray stone. With the head of the Dita, I smoothed the ground in front of the stones. Angling the stick's toe, I dug a pit into the bank directly in front of the stone line, removing leaves, twigs, and rocks. I knelt in the pit and faced my stones. Supported by the earth, I called out the names Jake, Brian, Lily, Conor, Diane, Debbie, Gwen, Marianna, Steven, Stacey and told them what I had not been able to say as their therapist: how I loved them, how I longed to do it all over again and be better for them, how I wished we could know each other for many long years. I told them I felt blessed by their gifts, their very lives.

In blackness on Stacey's last night I gathered the quartz and granite in my pockets. When the dark moments come, this is what compels us: to gather what we can—rocks, stones, granite, quartz, anything to hold on to—to balance the darkness ahead and the pain within.

The path wound ahead. I leaned on the Dita and moved slowly, looking alternately at the ground and forward, each step important as I walked the stones home.

Stacey died nine hours later, unconscious, at three forty-three a.m., watched by a nurse while her aunt rested.

23
Last Day

I read once about a village in England that chose to close its borders to visitors once the plague had come within its walls. The village's minister convinced his flock that to quarantine themselves would ensure that they would pass bubonic plague on to no one other than themselves. In so doing, they would protect strangers who would have come to their markets and extended family members who would have visited; and they would guarantee that each one in the village who became diseased would die in the arms of someone he or she knew, a neighbor or a kinsman. The earl of the county agreed to have food and supplies dropped at a rock wall bordering the village until the plague passed. No one who was ill was cast out; no one who was healthy allowed in. At the end of the year two-thirds of the village had died, yet not one of them had caused death outside the village. They stood together, held their line, facing a cancer of their time.

Stacey's funeral was held in a suburban church near the high school she had attended. The church was a massive, domed building with stone and marble floors, and no one could enter it without making their presence known; even rubber-soled shoes squeaked on the highly polished surface. Eighty-five pews lined each side of the church's main aisle. At the head of the last two pews were twin baptismal fonts. Four and a half feet high and carved out of yellow cast stone, they held the holy water into which we all dipped our hands. Even those who were not churchgoers felt the pull of immersing their fingers, then making the sign of the cross, for I saw not one person enter without doing so.

Nearly three hundred children and their parents came. I sat in the back row on the left with the team from the hospital. It was the only time I had ever seen an entire team—chief resident, resident, primary nurse, psychologist, and social worker—attend a funeral together. After the funeral I would say good-bye to these people. I would drive to the hospital, deliver my files to Donna for next year's interns, return my keys and pager, and copy down the numbers and addresses of my clients, just in case we would need each other in the future. But for this last moment, we were still a team.

Stacey's father was brought in a limousine to the funeral fifteen minutes late; we had already heard two psalms and the first eulogy. Wheelchair-bound, body and face contorted, Tim waved to each of us. "Hi. Look friends from the hospital," he said to his sister, his voice tranquilized and even.

Kara wheeled him to the back row, opposite us, and whispered to Scott, "He thinks he is at a wedding; the coffin would confuse him." Scott went to sit with Tim while the priest invited us to stand. As a group we rose and opened our books to lift our voices. "Morning Has Broken" began to echo through the high mahogany archways. We looked forward and faced Stacey's coffin. Draped in a simple white cloth, it seemed from this distance a dim star against the church's cavernous dark wood and black-clothed mourners. Behind the coffin stood the altar, and rising behind it three enormous tapestries were suspended—woven murals of dark angels falling, innocents praying, doves circling, and sunbeams breaking through storm clouds, their hues of rose, gold, pink, and apricot embracing the archangels Uriel, Michael, Raphael, and Gabriel who carried placid, pale children up and up and up.

April, 2006. I wish I could offer you the actual particulars of the children I got to know. How this one braided her hair and that one loved bears. How one would watch the needles going in, and another would close her eyes and dream aloud with me of a land far away. As a psychologist I cannot of course; the real identities, medical and personal details of my clients remain, as always, private to me. But we each long to name exactly what it is that makes the children we love unique and to share them with the world, even if the children die. It is why we tell their stories over and over again. Why when family members gather, the photographs come out, the anecdotes, the same funny moments are repeated—to help us all remember, to hold on to what was precious.

As a therapist or a physician this cannot happen in the same way. Our grief and longing are bounded by the nature of our professions and carried in a narrow inner space. I have come to accept this and know that it is alright—the children we treat live on in our bones. Their looks, their laughter, their idiosyncrasies are held within and help to shape our hearts and the lives of those we touch. They are not forgotten. Our children are not forgotten.

Epilogue
The Time Is Now

In the middle of the night, minister Frederick Buechner wrote in *The Hungering Dark,* the phone rings and we are asked to answer. We are asked to step deeply into life and respond to its capricious nature. Cancer, disease, tragedy, trauma, great joy—they come to each of us in their own time. Will we answer with our lives? Buechner wonders. Will we answer with our hearts awakened and open?

I say this, the phone rings always. The opportunity to answer is present always. How do we, how do any of us respond to the challenge of loving what is mortal?

More than ten years have passed since I left the hospital. Three of my close friends—Sue, Etta, and Libby—have died from various cancers, my husband, Jonathan, has survived Hodgkin's lymphoma, and my life yaws with each new diagnosis. I counsel adults, volunteer at my children's school and in the community, work the negotiations of marriage on a daily basis, exercise when I can, and write.

I carry the children with me. A necklace of gems—they shimmer only for me until I tell their stories and then they are alive to whomever I am with, reminding us of how grief is not something we get through or get over but rather a swell that is reshaped with each rise and pull. But there is more than grief here. There is a truth that both hurts and heals with its sharpness: You may never know who's going to get hit by the next bus, as Marianna said, but the life bus is already here. Draw, Antonio, draw, and do not waste time.

Life is something I have learned to seek. I take my children to the river park where the Housatonic measures one foot, four inches and eddies without rush. Jesse stands on slimy stones, listens for clunk and plop and plink as he disassembles the rock pile I make for him. He spies frogs and small fish we name "scooters" and asks how fish cuddle with their mommies when they don't have arms. My daughter, Raphaela, the elder, collects feathers, pebbles, chewed straws, and dead bugs. Jammed into her pockets, they are tagged with orders not to be washed, sorted, looked at, or in any manner touched by any other member of the family.

We eat yogurt, pudding, and chips on an old blanket with torn satin lining, and I wash Jesse's three-year-old hands in the still pool the river makes between stones braced by a fallen maple. We lie on our backs to name clouds, and on this day everything he sees is "hippopotamus" and everything my daughter sees is too fuzzy to name. She prefers ground to sky and as she rakes the earth for treasures she spouts accomplishments: how high she swings, how far she jumps, how long she stretches.

One day they will hear about the children from the hospital, and others, and Raphaela and Jesse will learn that they, too, will not be forgotten. I will assure them that their stories will live on in the lives they touch and their teachings will help others wake up to the importance of the lives they are already living. Every day counts, Steven reminds us, and I echo in response, each child counts.

We prepare to leave. My children and I carry home a leaf for Jonathan, a dried frog leg, walking stick branches, and yogurt cups. I am ordered to lick the cups clean, then fill them with river mud so that their special rocks, Jesse's yellow and peach oval and Raphaela's granite shard, can rest at night on soil they know. This is their work for now, to come close to the world and bring it home.

We say good-bye to the river, the trees, the grass, the fish, and the clouds, walking a three-year-old's pace back to the car. Behind my children I see Mary Oliver's black river of loss and ahead of them Buechner's call in the night and between those images a knowing that no one travels through life unscathed; to love each other in the face of such truth is a great task, a staircase worth climbing as Gwen might have said, with or without a leg here or there. "Spend it all," Dillard wrote. "Shoot it, play it, lose it, all, right away, every time." The time is now.

Appendix

National Resources for Childhood and Adult Cancer

American Cancer Society
1599 Clifton Road N.E.
Atlanta, GA 30329
1-800-ACS-2345
www.cancer.org

The Candlelighters Childhood Cancer Foundation
National Office
P.O. Box 498
Kensington, MD 20895-0498
1-800-366-2223
www.candlelighters.org

The Compassionate Friends, Inc.
P.O. Box 3696
Oak Brook, IL 60522-3696
1-877-969-0010
www.compassionatefriends.com

The Hole in the Wall Gang Camp
565 Ashford Center Rd.
Ashford, CT 06278
1-860-429-3444
www.holeinthewallgang.org

National Cancer Institute
NCI Public Inquiries Office
6116 Executive Blvd.
Room 3036A
Bethesda, MD 20892-8322
1-800-422-6237
www.cancer.gov

The National Childhood Cancer Foundation
Headquarters Office
4600 East West Highway, #600
Bethesda, MD 20814-3457
1-240-235-2200
www.curesearch.org

Bibliography

Barrows, Anita, and Joanna Macy. *Rilke's Book of Hours.* New York: Riverhead Books, 1996.

Berlin, Richard M. *How JFK Killed My Father.* Long Beach, Calif.: Pearl Editions, 2004.

Bly, Robert. *The Kabir Book.* Boston: Beacon Press, 1993.

Bombeck, Erma. *I Want to Grow Hair, I Want to Grow Up, I Want to Go to Boise.* New York: Harper & Row, 1989.

Buechner, Frederick. *The Hungering Dark.* New York: Harper & Row, 1969.

Dillard, Annie. *The Writing Life.* New York: Harper & Row, 1989.

Frost, Robert. *North of Boston.* New York: Henry Holt and Company, 1915.

Hilfiker, David. *Healing the Wounds.* New York: Pantheon Books, 1985.

Kidder, Tracy. *Mountains Beyond Mountains.* New York: Random House, 2003.

Naomi-Remen, Rachel. *Kitchen Table Wisdom.* New York: Penguin Putnam, 1996.

Oliver, Mary. *American Primitive.* Boston: Little, Brown and Company, 1983.

Selzer, Richard. *Mortal Lessons, Notes on the Art of Surgery.* New York: Harcourt Inc., 1987.

Siegel, Bernie S. *Love, Medicine & Miracles*. New York: Harper & Row, 1986.

Whyte, David. *Fire in the Earth*. Langley, Wash.: Many Rivers Press, 1992.

Acknowledgments

To my husband, Jonathan Kramer, who believed in my writing long before I did and who holds such wisdom in his great loving heart.

To my mother and father, Antoinette Sirois and Al Sirois, who awakened in me the two fundamental pillars of my life, a love of education and faith in the divine.

To the women who have loved me through it all, Chris Barash, Cynthia Berman, Alex Childs, Jane Ciepiela, Dawn Collins, Rosemary DeCroce, Danielle Driscoll, Kathy Fraker, Nancy Frumer-Styron, Izzy Lenihan, Debbie Little, Judy Marz, Judy Moss, Pat Neptune, Diane Rossman, Karen Rutschmann, Stacey Sabol, Andrea Schmitt, Nancy Stoll, and Amy Taylor, for your unending friendships.

To Myrna Hammerling and Elie Hammerling, for the constancy of your care.

To my mentors, Michelle Gillett and Patricia Lee Lewis, for your beauty, and your courage in finding language large enough to embrace our world.

To my writing buddies, Rich Berlin, Amy Brentano, and Susanne King, for your gorgeous, powerful words and your faith that I would find mine.

To my writing group, Barbara Bartle, Patti Crane, Laurie Epstein, Chris Erb, Florence Grende, Susan Hartung, Maggie Howard,

Fern Leslie, Megan Moore, and Wendy Noyes for keeping the flames in each other alive.

To Harvey Zimbler, M.D. for every thoughtful comment and playful moment.

To Jackie Malone, for your careful, kind, wise suggestions.

To my healers, Libby Barker, Rosalyn Bruyere, Jim Leone, and Fran Lippmann, for your belief in me and in the work we are all trying to do.

To Nina Ryan who made it happen.

To my relatives and in-laws, for loving each other, and me, and for keeping your hearts and kitchens open to those I love.

To my brothers, Joe Sirois and John Sirois, for the safety of knowing we will always be there for each other.

To my children, Raphaela and Jesse, for every wonderous, challenging moment and for the touch of you in the world.

To my tribe in the ethers—thank you.

A Note on the Author

Maria Sirois, Psy.D., is a licensed clinical psychologist who trained as a volunteer at the New England Deaconess Mind/Body Clinic, where she assisted in teaching meditation, stress management, and self-care to patients with chronic and terminal illness, and at the Dana-Farber Cancer Institute, both in Boston, Massachusetts. Dr. Sirois was a lecturer for several years at Canyon Ranch in Lenox, Massachusetts, and is a frequent keynote speaker and presenter on health and spirituality at regional businesses, colleges, hospitals, and religious institutions. This is her first book. She lives with her husband and two children in western Massachusetts.